ALL IN

ORPHAN CARE

ALL IN

ORPHAN CARE

*Exploring the call to care for vulnerable
children and families*

REVISED EDITION

JASON JOHNSON

ALL IN
ORPHAN CARE

Published in the United States by Credo House Publishers,
a division of Credo Communications, LLC, Grand Rapids, Michigan
credohousepublishers.com

For more information, please visit *jasonjohnsonblog.com*

ISBN: 978-1-625861-27-6

Cover and interior design by Karl Dinkler

Printed in the United States of America
Revised Edition

For more information, visit *allinorphancare.com*

> *It's the mercy of God that He doesn't show us everything that will unfold in the foster care and adoption journey the moment we first say "yes" to it; all the hard would be too unbearable and all the good would be too unbelievable.*

JASON JOHNSON

ReFraming Foster Care

CONTENTS

A STORY OF REDEMPTION

—

Mark Tennant

In 1972, there were 320,000 children in foster care — of which I was one. At the age of 11, a story of unspeakable darkness began to unfold in my life. An alcoholic, violent man in my home led me to endure emotional, physical and sexual abuse. My only outlet was to hope, pray and wait for love and security to come from a seemingly powerless mother. In the end, she ran toward the abuser rather than to me, the abused.

I was left alone to tend to the needs of my younger sister, and I would become her protector and defender until the day when, through court intervention, I was removed from my home and separated from her and everything else I had ever known. I left with nothing. One morning, I got on the bus and left for school having no idea that by that evening I would be placed in foster care never having said goodbye. I would never return to live with my family under the same roof.

For the next couple of years, I was moved from home to home in foster care with no real certainty about the future, until the day the people I now call Mom and Dad stepped into my life. For the next five years, before turning 18, Bill and Joan Mack, and all of their extended family, poured themselves into my life. They gave of themselves to me and introduced me to a God who would give me a future and a hope, always reassuring me that I would be their son and I would have a family and a home with them forever, no matter what. While I may have left their home at 18, I did not leave their family. Today, they are my parents and the grandparents to my kids. They are mine and I am theirs. Forever.

Yes, in 1972, I was one of those kids; but in 1992, I founded Arrow Child & Family Ministries to help those kids who were just like me.

Over the past 24 years, Arrow has served thousands upon thousands of children in foster care and has helped many of them find their forever family through adoption. It has been a wonderful experience to not only to see God's redemptive work in my own life but in the lives of many other children and families. God has done this for us through Jesus. We are therefore compelled to do the same for them.

I believe that over the next few generations, those within the Church will link arms with others in their community. They will stand in the gap for children and families in crisis and with uncertain futures by providing the capacity, quality and stability for which the Church is uniquely called and equipped. This is my hope and dream.

Yes, in 1972, I was one of those kids; but in 1992, I founded Arrow Child & Family Ministries to help those kids who were just like me.

I want to personally say, "Thank you." Thank you for standing in the gap for kids like me. I am confident that I would not be where I am today had someone like you not intervened on my behalf. You are making an eternal impact in the lives of children and families far more than you could possibly imagine. Thank you for being willing to be used by God in the lives of these kids so that a world that is orphaned from Him might have a profound taste of what redemption, restoration, hope and healing can look like.

God is still writing stories on the pages of kids' hearts. Bill and Joan Mack chose to become a part of mine. Will you choose to become a part of one of the many others?

My thoughts and prayers are with you as you consider this calling,

Mark Tennant

HOW TO USE THIS STUDY

—

NO LEADER NECESSARY

Our hope is that this workbook is as accessible and user friendly as possible so that any group could pick it up and use it, whether there is a designated "leader" or not. The material is written so that members of the group can share responsibilities to read and help navigate everyone else through different sections.

HEAD, HEART & HANDS PARADIGM

A unique feature of this study is what we call the "Fully-Integrated Paradigm: Head, Heart and Hands." This approach to the study seeks to balance the attention we are paying to what we must learn (head), what we must feel (heart) and what we must do (hands).

Before beginning the first session, have the group read the "Head, Heart and Hands" Paradigm material found on page 17.

SESSION OUTLINES

Each session is organized around five primary sections: PRAY, CONNECT, GROW, DISCUSS and REFLECT.

Here's a brief description of each:

PRAY — Begin each group meeting with prayer. Give each group member the opportunity to share any particular requests they would like the group to pray for. This is an important time to encourage one another and focus your hearts and minds on what God may have in store during your meeting.

CONNECT — Take this opportunity to catch up on what's going on in each other's lives. How has your week been? Did anything out of the ordinary or particularly interesting happen? Use the questions in this section to help gear the group's thoughts around the theme of the study.

GROW — This is the study portion. Each session includes scripture passages, commentary and discussion questions to read. As you work through this section, either a) assign one person to facilitate the whole section or b) ask different group members to facilitate different parts.

DISCUSS — As you close each group meeting spend 5-10 minutes discussing main ideas and application points from the study. What stood out to you the most? Why? This section is intended to provide the group the opportunity to process and think aloud together before leaving.

REFLECT — Each group member is encouraged to personally process and apply some of the things they are learning. This reflection resource can also be something to look back on one day so participants can see all God has done since they began working through this material. Some space to write is provided in this workbook, or you can use your own journal if more space is required.

WHY THE CHURCH MUST CARE FOR THE VULNERABLE

—

Jason Johnson

It was never God's intent for children to be without a family. Among the unending evidences that we live in a fatally sin-scarred world, this specific consequence particularly pains the heart of God. This is why Scripture says He "executes justice for the fatherless" (Deuteronomy 10:18) and assumes the role of "the father of the fatherless" (Psalm 68:5). This is the heart of God, a good, loving and gracious Father.

If you were to read the Bible from the very beginning to the very end, several themes would surface that are consistent throughout the narrative of Scripture. Things like God's power, God's mercy and God's faithfulness, or man's weakness, rebellion and ultimate need for redemption. These and many others fill the pages of both the Old and New Testaments, telling a beautiful story of God's relentless pursuit of His people whom He loves.

Yet, of all the themes to be found within the pages of Scripture, one that shines with unparalleled clarity and stands with an unmatched prominence and stature is this: God secures and protects the rights of the helpless and the hopeless. From the beginning of time to the very end, God intercedes on behalf of the marginalized and offers to them the abundance of His sufficiency. That which particularly pains His heart unequivocally drives his actions. He sets His pursuit on filling the empty, embracing the marginalized and healing the broken and destitute in Jesus' name. The Apostle Paul in 2 Corinthians 8:9 articulates it this way:

> *"... you know the grace of our Lord Jesus Christ, that though he was rich, yet for your sake he became poor, so that you by his poverty might become rich."*

This is the gospel, that while we were empty and isolated, the riches of the grace of God in Jesus fully filled us and freely welcomed us. We simply cannot escape this theme in Scripture, but it doesn't end there...

The Bible expects that what particularly pains God's heart would particularly pain ours, and what unequivocally drives His actions would without hindrance drive ours. The benefits of God's abundance poured into us when we were empty and destitute do not terminate on us. Rather, they are to be extended into the lives of others around us. So now, following the pattern of how God consistently works, we are called to "give justice to the weak and fatherless" (Psalm 82:3) and to "seek justice, correct oppression [and] bring justice to the fatherless" (Isaiah 1:16-17). As seekers of justice and correctors of oppression, **we care for vulnerable children and families because we have been greatly cared for in Jesus;** we seek justice for them because justice has been won for us in Jesus; we step into their brokenness because Jesus sacrifically stepped into ours; we adopt, because as the

Apostle Paul writes, Jesus came "so that we might receive adoption" (Galatians 4:5). His work on our behalf becomes the motivation behind our work on theirs.

This leads us to the clarion passage in the New Testament speaking to our care of the most vulnerable around us. In the Christian life, we can demonstrate our faith in God in a variety of ways – i.e. prayer, giving, worship, serving, etc. The means by which our faith can express itself are seemingly endless and full of possibilities. Yet, in James 1:27, we are told that of all the measures by which our faith can be demonstrated, caring for the vulnerable in their distress ranks among the highest and purest.

> *"Religion that is pure and undefiled before God, the Father, is this: to visit orphans and widows in their affliction, and to keep oneself unstained from the world."*

Why would God hold the care of the vulnerable in such high regard? Why does He rank it among the highest expressions of our faith? Perhaps because **caring for the vulnerable is one of the purest and most undefiled demonstrations of the heart of God and expressions of the work of Jesus in the gospel this world will ever see.** We'll discuss James 1:27 in greater detail later in this study, but for now the main idea is this: If the gospel is ultimately the story of those who were empty and isolated from God being brought into His family by the work of Jesus, then our care for the vulnerable and orphaned is a beautiful continuation of the redemption story of God and a vivid demonstration of the love of Jesus extended through us. Again, our care of the vulnerable is rooted in God's care of us through Jesus – it begins not with the child "out there" who needs a family but with the child in us that has been given one in Jesus.

This is the foundation our study is built upon – God's heart for the marginalized, the theology of God interceding into our story and our gospel-centered response to the need around us. It is our great hope that as the gospel is pressed into our hearts more deeply, our desire to demonstrate that redemption story to others would grow more widely. Our encouragement to you is to discern how the Holy Spirit may lead you in light of the truths you will discover together through this study, and that in doing so you may be stretched to dream bigger dreams and believe greater things for how, and when and where God may want to use you to seek justice, correct oppression and care for the most vulnerable and marginalized around you.

The Head, Heart & Hands Paradigm

THE HEAD, HEART & HANDS PARADIGM

—

As Christians, we are called to love and serve God with every aspect of our being. In Mark 12:30, Jesus quotes an Old Testament commandment when He says, "You shall love the Lord your God with all your heart and with all your soul and with all your mind and with all your strength." Scripture is not compartmentalizing the ways in which we love and serve God, as if we can turn the soul off and move into the mind category, or momentarily set aside the strength compartment while we operate out of the heart. Rather, the Old Testament command quoted in the New Testament by Jesus is a timeless, holistic one, meant to illustrate that no part of who we are is exempt from being used to know and love God, and all parts are used together as one in serving Him.

To simplify the idea, think of the Christian faith as being rooted in our knowing, loving and serving God with our HEAD (mind), our HEART (soul) and our HANDS (strength).

These three dimensions – head, heart and hands – are not mutually exclusive or isolated from one another. Rather, each feeds and sustains the others by helping to form a unified and "fully integrated" self.

When taken in isolation, our faith becomes fragmented, over-accentuating one dimension to the neglect of the others.

For example, if our faith is primarily HEAD-based, we may rely heavily on knowledge of God without ever having a truly close or intimate relationship with Him. Or, if our faith is primarily HANDS-based we may do a lot for God but not ever form a strong grasp on what we believe about Him as Scripture teaches. Or, if our faith is primarily HEART-based we may experience very emotional, mystical moments with God that are not rooted in an understanding of the truth of who He is or are detached from a biblically grounded relationship with Him.

Jesus exposes the fragmented faith of people on several occasions in Scripture, with one of the most notable being found in Matthew 7:21-23:

> *"Not everyone who says to me, 'Lord, Lord,' will enter the kingdom of heaven, but the one who does the will of my Father who is in heaven. On that day many will say to me, 'Lord, Lord, did we not prophesy in your name, and cast out demons in your name, and do many mighty works in your name?' And then will I declare to them, 'I never knew you; depart from me...'*

In other words, many will rely on the works of their HANDS only to find that their HEARTS were never close to Him. Some will give their time and energy to the things of God but will never actually give their lives to Him. This is a fragmented faith that in the end leads to missing out on what God has in store for us.

We could go on. The point, however, is that by themselves none of these dimensions can do justice to the fullness of the capacity God has given us to know and love and serve Him with our whole selves. Our faith must not be fragmented, but rather a fully integrated make-up of the whole of who we are otherwise our aptitude (head), affections (heart) and actions (hands) can never be truly utilized to the capacity God intended.

FULLY-INTEGRATED ORPHAN CARE

Why spend so much time on knowing, loving and serving God in a fully integrated way? Because this will act as the framework through which we respond to His mandate to care for the vulnerable and orphaned around us. At the end of the day it's not enough to know God's heart on the matter (head) and never do anything about it (hands), or to feel strongly about the issues of justice (heart) with no real grasp on the biblical call to care for others (head) and no real actions that are doing anything about it (hands). It's one thing to care about the vulnerable; it's an entirely different thing to care for them. One is head or heart centered; the other drives the actions of our hands. This is the intent of our study — to identify how each of us are called not just to care *about*, but to care *for* the vulnerable and orphaned.

Even now as we begin this study, some hold to right beliefs about orphan care but their actions are not following suit. Some are very emotionally invested but do not have a firm grasp on what God has to say on the matter. Others are sincerely concerned about the issues and are involved in matters of justice but are being driven by their own efforts or recognition, not the heart of God. Wherever you may be now, the intent of this study is to lead us all into a further developing and maturing understanding of what it means for us as individuals, groups, churches and communities to be fully-integrated in our faith and lives.

At the end of the day, if we pursue the care of the vulnerable and orphaned in a fragmented way, our right thoughts will only get us so far, our strong emotions will last but a while, and our good works will eventually become exhausting efforts. The only sustainable way for us to respond by faith to what God is calling us to do is to be fully integrated in our approach, with right beliefs, right emotions and right actions working in harmony with one another. Then, when one part is weak (say for instance the work is especially grueling and we are tempted to quit), the others will help guide and sustain (our beliefs that the work is pleasing to God and worth it will motivate us to keep going).

Throughout this study, you will be asked to use the HEAD-HEART-HANDS paradigm to apply the truths we are learning and discussing in each session – i.e. What biblical truth do we learn from this? How does what we are discussing move you and make you feel? What are you going to do in response to what we have learned together? This is a critical component of this study and will act as a starting point for what will prove to be some very encouraging and helpful dialogue.

—

A CLEAR AND COMPELLING "WHY"

—

God sees hards places and broken people and moves towards them, not away from them.

PRAY

—

As you gather the group together, begin with prayer. Each group member should have the opportunity to share any particular requests they would like the group to pray for. Use this time as an opportunity to encourage one another and focus your hearts and minds on what God may have in store during your time together.

CONNECT

—

If any group members do not already know each other, introduce yourselves and share a little of your story. Answer questions like:

- *Where were you born?*
- *What brought you to this city?*
- *Are you married? (If so, for how long? How did you meet?)*
- *Do you have kids? (If so, how many?)*
- *What do you do for a living?*
- *Etc.*

Spend the next 5-10 minutes connecting as a group. Catch up on what's going on in each other's lives.

- *How has your week been?*
- *Did anything out of the ordinary or particularly interesting happen?*
- *Is anything coming up for you between now and the next group meeting that you want group members to know?*

Why Are You Here?

During this first session, it is important to discuss why everyone has chosen to attend this group and go through a study on caring for vulnerable children and families. As much as you are able, share:

- *Where are you in the process of fostering, adopting or finding ways to support?*

- *Why did you feel particularly led by God to go through this study?*

- *What do you hope to gain from going through this study and being part of this group?*

GROW

—

Before You Begin: Read the "Why The Church Must Care For the Vulnerable" found on page 13 together as a group. Either a) have different members read portions out loud or, b) give each member a few minutes to read silently on their own. As time allows, discuss the main points of the introduction and familiarize yourself with some of the key scripture passages.

- *What do these passages teach us about God's heart for justice?*

- *What do we learn about His actions towards the marginalized and destitute?*

- *What do these passages reveal about God's expectations of us?*

- *How does our seeking of justice and correcting of oppression put God's heart for these things on display in this world?*

The Gospel is Our "Why"

As we saw in the study introduction, the care of the orphaned and vulnerable is a response to the heart of God to bring justice to the marginalized and families to the fatherless. It is allowing what drives His actions towards the vulnerable to drive ours in similar fashion.

Of all the evidences that this world is not as it should be, none seem to be more paramount to the heart of God than when injustices rule, oppression runs rampant and children are left to fend for themselves without the loving and nurturing support of a healthy family. This at the core of our "why". Let's explore in more depth...

Transformation of status for the lowly, the humanly hopeless, as they experience the hand of God reaching into their situation, is possibly the most pervasive theme of biblical writings.

– Dallas Willard

READ:

1 John 3:16,18 —
> *This is how we know what love is: Jesus Christ laid down his life for us. And we ought to lay down our lives for our brothers and sisters... let us not love with words or speech, but with actions and in truth.*

The work of Jesus on our behalf compels us to work on behalf of others. Why would we step into the hard? Why would we lean into the broken? Why would we open our families to the traumatic and difficult? Because that's what Jesus has done for us. We lay our lives down for others because He first sacrificially laid down His life for us.

He saw our brokenness and embraced us in our weakness, adopted us into His family and changed the course of our lives forever.

This beautiful picture of the gospel, and its vivid implications in our care of the orphaned and vulnerable, plays itself out through two primary aspects of theology: 1) Our Adoption; 2) His Incarnation.

1) The Doctrine of Our Adoption

READ:

John 1:12-13 —

> *See what great love the Father has lavished on us, that we should be called children of God! And that is what we are!*

The hinge upon which this entire new relationship with God has been formed is beautifully illustrated in scripture through the continuous use of the word "adoption". Passages such as:

Ephesians 1:5 —

> *He predestined us for **adoption** as sons through Jesus Christ.*

Romans 8:15 —

> *You did not receive the spirit of slavery to fall back into*
> *fear, but you have received the Spirit of **adoption** as sons,*
> *by whom we cry, "Abba! Father!"*

We were once outside the family of God but now, through the work

of Christ on our behalf, have been adopted as dearly loved sons and daughters. The theology of our adoption helps form the basis of our "why." Why would we care for orphaned and vulnerable children by bringing them into our families? Because that's what Christ has done for us. But it doesn't end there…

2) The Doctrine of His Incarnation

The word "incarnation" literally means to assume human form. The doctrine of Christ's incarnation speaks to God stepping into humanity, wrapping Himself in flesh and living completely and fully as both God and man. It's most notably recognized at Christmas with the birth of Jesus, yet its implications are far more pervasive than just on December 25th of every year.

READ:

Matthew 1:22-23 —

> *All this took place to fulfill what the Lord had said through*
> *the prophet: "The virgin will conceive and give birth to a*
> *son, and they will call Him Immanuel" (which means "God*
> *with us").*

The incarnation tells us that **God sees hard places and broken peoples and moves towards them**, not away. He is "with us". He wrapped Himself up in our brokenness, carried our brokenness to the Cross, and was broken by our brokenness so that we don't have to be broken anymore. God saw us in our plight and moved towards us, not away. That's the gospel.

The theology of Christ's incarnation helps form the basis of our "why." Why would we immerse — or incarnate — ourselves into hard and broken places? Because that's what Christ has done for us.

The implications of the doctrine of incarnation are broad. The opportunities for each unique individual to "incarnate" themselves into hard and broken places are endless and full of creativity. This moves the conversation beyond just foster care, adoption or orphan care in some capacity — and speaks to a renewed posture and perspective towards the world around us in all matters of justice, mercy and sacrifice.

♦ *What other implications does you think this renewed posture has in our lives?*

♦ *What applications can you see it applying to besides the obvious foster care, adoption, orphan care and family support?*

This leads us to one of the most commonly referenced bible verses when it comes to caring for orphans, engaging in foster care and adopting children into our families. Let's explore...

READ:

James 1:27 —

> *Religion that is pure and undefiled before God, the Father,*
> *is this: to visit orphans and widows in their affliction, and*
> *to keep oneself unstained from the world.*

This verse is used very often. Let's break it down a bit:

- *The word "religion" in this context literally means "an*
  outward display of something that's inwardly true." That's
  what we're talking about - an outward display of the gospel
  that's inwardly true in us.

- *The word "visit" means to "move towards, step towards, get*
  involved with". Not avoid or isolate, but engage.

- *The reference to "orphans and widows" is representative of*
  the most vulnerable people groups in James' context.

So, let's consider that James 1:27 might not be as "prescriptive" as it is "descriptive". James isn't isolating his concern - and ultimately God's concern - to just orphans and widows. He's not necessarily giving us a prescription (orphans and widows only), but is rather describing what one of the purest and most undefiled demonstrations of the gospel looks like - by using orphans and widows as respresentatives of the most aggregiously vulnerable groups of people in his cultural context.

Today this could also include the homeless, poor, victims of trafficking, etc. James wouldn't say to us "No, God doesn't care about them." Instead he would say, "Yes! That's who this verse is about too!"

In other words, James is saying that one of the purest and

most undefiled outward demonstrations of the gospel which is inwardly true in us is to see hard places and broken people and move towards them, not away from them. Why? Because this is exactly what Jesus has done for us!

Questions to Consider:

- *Why does James suggest that giving involved with the hard and broken so uniquely puts the gospel on display?*

- *How is the message of moving towards hard and broken places contrary to the cultural narrative we are surrounded by? What does the world say we should do when with hard and broken things? (Hint: Think of words like avoid, isolate, insulate, etc.)*

- *What keeps us from moving towards hard places and broken people?*

Let my heart be broken by the things that break the heart of God.

— *Bob Pierce, Founder of World Vision*

READ:

Galatians 4:4-5 —

> *When the fullness of time had come, God sent forth his Son, born of a woman, born under the law, to redeem those who were under the law, so that we might receive adoption as sons.*

In this passage the Apostle Paul reiterates the incarnation of

Christ and beautifully ties it into God's redemptive pursuit of humanity to make us His children. He says Jesus was *"born of a woman"* **(incarnation)** in order *"that we might receive adoption"* **(adoption)** into His family. The beautiful coming together of adoption and incarnation produces some incredible things in our lives, which we will explore in the next session!

THREE THINGS THE GOSPEL DOES:

1. **It Compels Us Into It** | The work of Jesus on our behalf becomes the primary motivation as to why we would work on theirs – He moved towards us, so we too move towards them.

2. **It Sustains Us in the Midst of It** | When the work of orphan care gets especially difficult, and we're left asking "Why are we doing this?" the gospel reminds us that the work is worth it — it gives meaning to the struggle and context to the difficulty.

3. **It is Put On Display Through It** | Caring for the orphaned and vulnerable is one of the purest and most undefiled demonstrations of the gospel the world will ever see.

The echoes of the gospel in orphan care are beautiful and vivid.

We cannot neglect the gospel as the source and sustenance of our "why". It is the beginning of our motivation, the sustaining power in the middle and the beauty put on display in the end.

DISCUSS

As you close your time together, spend 5-10 minutes processing the things you have learned and discussed. This is an especially important opportunity to share thoughts, feelings, questions, concerns or any resolutions you have made in response to your study.

1. *What truth or idea stood out to you most in this session? Why?*

2. *In your own words, describe the connection between the doctrines of our adoption and Christ's incarnation.*

3. *Why is it so important for us to understand the theology of the gospel as it pertains to our care of the vulnerable?*

REFLECT

As you reflect on the truths of this session and consider the personal implications for your own life, spend some time writing and praying through the following three questions:

1. *What are your hopes and expectations going into this process or continuing the process you have already begun?*

2. *As of right now, what does "caring for orphans" look like for you and/or your family?*

3. *Would you be willing to let God expand the parameters you have set? What fears, questions, anxieties or concerns do you have?*

REFLECTIVE WRITING

_____

_____

_____

_____

_____

_____

_____

_____

_____

_____

_____

_____

_____

_____

_____

_____

_____

_____

_____

_____

_____

ADDITIONAL SCRIPTURE TO USE IN PRAYER:

Galatians 4:1–7, Ephesians 1:11, Romans 8:9–17, 1 John 4:18–19

HEAD: *What biblical truth did you learn from this?*

_____

_____

HEART: *What do the ideas we are discussing make you think and feel?*

_____

_____

HANDS: *What are you going to do in response to what we have learned?*

_____

_____

THE THEOLOGY OF OUR REDEMPTION

—

Orphan care, like the Gospel, is a multi-generational story of redemption.

PRAY

—

As you gather the group together, begin with prayer. Each group member should have the opportunity to share any particular requests they would like the group to pray for. Use this time as an opportunity to encourage one another and focus your hearts and minds on what God may have in store during your time together.

CONNECT

—

Spend the next 5-10 minutes connecting as a group. Catch up on what's going on in each other's lives.

- ♦ *How has your week been?*
- ♦ *Did anything out of the ordinary or particularly interesting happen?*
- ♦ *Is anything coming up for you between now and the next group meeting that you want group members to know?*

In Session 1, we learned that the core of our motivation to care for the orphaned and vulnerable is the heart of God demonstrated through the gospel on our behalf. In this session, we will explore how the gospel redeems our pasts, presents and futures. In light of that we will discuss the implications as they pertain to caring for kids from hard places.

To begin, have members of the group briefly share how Jesus has changed their pasts, presents and futures.

Examples:

- *Jesus freed me from my past addiction, has given me a present reality of sobriety and protected me from a future that would have been plagued by the consequences of continuing in that broken pattern.*

- *My past was marked by broken relationships, but God has been gracious to give me a strong marriage and/or friendships today. I'm committed to commitment in these relationships forever.*

- *I experienced some horrendous things in my past, but God has graciously carried me through them all. I believe He wants to use my past hurts to help minister to others in the future.*

GROW

–

A Multi-Generational Story

The imagery of adoption is used throughout Scripture to paint a vivid picture of the Gospel — God's rescuing and redeeming love for us in Jesus. Our salvation, or introduction into the family of God through Jesus, is presented as a multi-generational story of hope – breaking **past** cycles of brokenness, securing a new **present** reality and altering our **future** trajectory for all eternity. Because of the work of Christ on our behalf, we who were once isolated have been brought into the family of God as sons and daughters – and this changes everything forever!

The deepest and strongest foundation of adoption is located not in the act of humans adopting humans, but in God adopting humans. And this act is not part of His ordinary providence in the world; it is at the heart of the gospel.

– John Piper

As we discussed in Session 1, the doctrines of our adoption and Christ's incarnation act as the basis of our care of the most vulnerable around us (review that discussion if necessary). In this session we will explore the implications of the gospel in our lives and the new story it writes - past, present and future:

READ:

Galatians 4:4-7 —

> **4** *But when the fullness of time had come, God sent forth his Son, born of woman, born under the law,* **5** *to redeem those who were under the law, so that we might receive adoption as sons.* **6** *And because you are sons, God has sent the Spirit of his Son into our hearts, crying, "Abba! Father!"* **7** *So you are no longer a slave, but a son, and if a son, then an heir through God.*

Adoption and Incarnation (v4)

* *In session 1 we briefly discussed how this verse brings together adoption and incarnation. Revisit that discussion before exploring its effects in our lives in vs.5-7.*

Past Redeemed (v5)

* *What does this verse say was the two-fold purpose of God incarnating Himself to this earth?*

♦ *The phrase "were under the law" is in the past tense – What does this communicate about the effect the work of Jesus has had on our past sin, guilt, shame, isolation from God, etc.?*

READ:

2 Corinthians 5:17 —

> *Therefore, if anyone is in Christ, he is a new creation. The old has passed away; behold, the new has come*

Psalm 103:12 —

> *... as far as the east is from the west, so far does he remove our transgressions from us.*

Romans 8:1 —

> *There is therefore now no condemnation for those who are in Christ Jesus.*

♦ *How far has God's forgiveness reached into our past?*

♦ *Why do you think so many struggle with still feeling "condemned"?*

<u>Point:</u> In Jesus, our past has been redeemed – we were once isolated and at odds with God...but Jesus has reconciled, renewed and brought us near. Our past is no longer a source of condemnation, but has now become a platform of celebration. We can look back and say, "Wow, look at what Jesus has done!" The gospel tells us that broken things don't have to be final things.

Present Secured (v6)

The term "Abba" is the Aramaic form of the word "Daddy" which denotes intimacy and affection. What does this verse teach us about where we stand with God positionally through the gospel? How does our present standing with Him contrast to where we once stood with Him in our sin (i.e. separated, condemned, etc.)?

Adoption is the highest privilege that the gospel offers.

– J.I. Packer

READ:

John 1:9-13 —

> ... to all who did receive him, who believed in his name, he gave the right to become children of God, who were born, not of blood nor of the will of the flesh nor of the will of man, but of God

James 1:17 —

> Every good gift and every perfect gift is from above, coming down from the Father of lights with whom there is no variation or shadow due to change.

James 1:17 —

> Which one of you, if his son asks him for bread, will give him a stone? Or if he asks for a fish, will give him a

serpent? If you then, who are evil, know how to give good gifts to your children, how much more will your Father who is in heaven give good things to those who ask him!

♦   *What benefits and privileges do we presently live under as children of God?*

♦   *How have we come about receiving those?*

Point: We live today with the full rights and privileges of being children of God. As our Father, He protects, provides, shows compassion and even disciplines us in love. We were once alienated, but now we are intimate. We do not come to Him with apprehension but with assurance, knowing we will always be accepted, listened to and loved by our "Abba." This is our present security.

Future Guaranteed (v7)

READ:

1 Peter 1:3-5 —

Blessed be the God and Father of our Lord Jesus Christ! According to his great mercy, he has caused us to be born again to a living hope through the resurrection of Jesus Christ from the dead, to an inheritance that is imperishable, undefiled, and unfading, kept in heaven for you, who by God's power are being guarded through faith for a salvation ready to be revealed in the last time.

Ephesians 1:13-14 —

In him you also, when you heard the word of truth, the gospel of your salvation, and believed in him, were sealed with the promised Holy Spirit, who is the guarantee of our inheritance until we acquire possession of it, to the praise of his glory.

Romans 8:15-17 —

For you did not receive the spirit of slavery to fall back into fear, but you have received the Spirit of adoption as sons, by whom we cry, "Abba! Father!" The Spirit himself bears witness with our spirit that we are children of God, and if children, then heirs—heirs of God and fellow heirs with Christ...

- *How should hope, assurance and confidence in the future change the way we live today?*
- *What are some practical examples you can give?*

Point: Our future in Christ is promised to be full of glory. It may not be without its difficulty along the way, but we can trust that no matter what happens around us, there is an inheritance waiting for us that cannot be taken away from us. The future trajectories of our lives have been eternally changed. We can look towards the future not in fear, but in hope.

The gospel is a multi-generational story of redemption. It breaks our past cycles, forms our new realities and offers us a future hope unburdened by the broken contexts from which we originated. God changes our names. He gives us new identities. He grants us the rights and privileges of being His sons and daughters. He secures our futures and changes the trajectory of our lives forever.

Why Talk About The Gospel So Much?

You may be asking this question – I thought this study was about caring for kids and families, so why are we spending so much time talking about the gospel? That's a great question! The answer is simple: Caring for the vulnerable does not begin with seeing the child "out there" who needs a family but with recognizing the child in us who's been given one in Jesus. The gospel in us is where we begin, but it does not terminate there. The end goal is for the story of the gospel in us to be declared and demonstrated through us into the lives of those around us – and in the interests of our particular study, into the lives of the most vulnerable among us.

As the gospel story of redemption is being told in our lives, we have the opportunity to see the same story brought to bear in theirs. **Caring for the vulnerable, like the gospel, is a multi-generational story of redemption** – it works to break past cycles of brokenness, form new realities of security and change future trajectories in beautifully profound, hard and redemptive ways.

Questions to Consider:

- *Where do you think you would be right now had Jesus not interceded in your life when He did?*

- *How can you intercede in the life of a child so that one day they may say, "I can't imagine where I would be right now had _____ not stepped into my life?"*

DISCUSS

As you close your time together, spend 5-10 minutes processing the things you have learned and discussed. This is an especially important opportunity to share thoughts, feelings, questions, concerns or any resolutions you have made in response to your study.

1. *What truth or idea stood out to you most in this session? Why?*

2. *In your own words, describe how the gospel and our care of the vulnerable are both "multi-generational" stories.*

3. *Why is it so important for us to understand the theology of the gospel as it pertains to our care of the vulnerable?*

REFLECT

As you reflect on the truths of this session and consider the personal implications for your own life, spend some time writing and praying through the following three questions:

1. *Looking back on your life, how do you see the faithfulness of God working through your past to bring you to the point where you are today?*

2. *If you could measure your current posture of worship towards Jesus and celebration in the gospel on a scale of 1-10, with 1 being near apathetic and 10 being pure adoration, where would you be right now? What are some specific things you can do to grow in your awareness of the gospel and affections for God?*

3. *In what ways do you need to actively take the "next steps" in demonstrating the gospel more widely to the most vulnerable around you?*

REFLECTIVE WRITING

_____

_____

_____

_____

_____

_____

_____

_____

_____

_____

_____

_____

_____

_____

_____

_____

_____

_____

_____

_____

_____

ADDITIONAL SCRIPTURE TO USE IN PRAYER:

Jeremiah 29:11–13; 2 Corinthians 9:8; 2 Peter 3:8–9; Nehemiah 1:4–11; Ephesians 1:18; John 1:1–5

HEAD: *What biblical truth did you learn from this?*

_____

_____

HEART: *What do the ideas we are discussing make you think and feel?*

_____

_____

HANDS: *What are you going to do in response to what we have learned?*

_____

_____

–

UNIMAGINABLY BETTER

–

David & Emily Gentiles
Foster and Adoptive Parents

What smooth dude brings up foster care on a first date? Well, I did. Fortunately, I didn't scare Emily away. It was more than delusions of grandeur or naive plans of kingdom greatness. She, too, had been prompted by the Lord that she and her someday husband would open their home to a little one that needed help, hope, and family.

Eight years into marriage and five years into our journey of infertility, I felt intensely that it was time to get the ball rolling. With a constant "wait" in her heart and the hope to have kids of our own first, Emily was more hesitant to begin the process. After being a part of a church where the pastor and a vast majority of our members were involved in orphan care, we were both wooed and convicted by the scriptures and the Holy Spirit that it was time. That summer we stepped into this new unknown together as ready as we knew how to be.

Our first week of foster caring was a roller coaster. On a Monday morning we received a call about a 5 month old that was going to be brought to our home that evening. Emily raced to Target to get the basics. We washed sheets, portioned out formula canisters, scrubbed bottles, and put his bed together. Our family drove down to be with us as we waited for him to arrive. We waited. And waited. And waited. Finally, around 10:30p I called our CPS contact to check in and she told me that they decided to place him with another family member and simply forgot to tell us.

Our home was filled with baby everything and no baby. We were stunned. We knew that this was part of the emotional risk that we submitted ourselves to, so we prayed and cried and tried to see God's hand weaving something good in our story. The next day we received another call for a placement that yet again didn't pan out. Deep breaths. Thursday of that same week we received a third call for two young brothers that would be with us later that same evening. And back to Target® we went for Fruit Loops® and bigger beds.

When the boys arrived they were very sweet and we were filled with compassion. However, within hours our world would be turned upside down. We learned later that the boys had come from a very violent and rage-filled home. We tried to put the puzzle pieces of their backstory together, even as our new nightly routine included hours of terror-filled shrieking. It would take 3 or more hours to help them drift off to sleep at bedtime and then around 2am the screaming would start. Night after night we were up with them into the late hours of the morning trying to console them as they threw punches at us and screamed and begged for their mother. Emily and I thought we were losing our minds. Many times we would call to the Lord for help, for comfort, for wisdom, and for rescue. I remember specifically one night around 2:30a asking the Lord to get me through the top of the hour and then we'd go from there.

After five weeks the boys were placed with their maternal grandparents. It was right and good for all of us. The day we dropped them off at the CPS office we felt a distinct heart gumbo of relief, loss, joy, and completion. We felt guilty because we were so very relieved that they had been placed back with their family. We felt loss because we weren't parents anymore, even if only foster parents. We felt joy because we'd completed the call to love those boys and care for them. While we wrestled with the mix, we knew we had been obedient.

A few months later and after some much-needed rest, we received an email blast from our agency describing an 8-month-old little boy named Royal. He was still in the foster care process, but he was in the "legal risk" category and CPS wanted him to be placed in an adoptive home. We put our names in the hat, knowing the selection process could take weeks if not months. Just a few days later extenuating circumstances caused his case to flip back to emergency placement and we were chosen by his caseworker in a matter of hours. On June 10th Royal came to our home. He was beautiful. His smile lit up the room. The moment we saw him we sensed that he would be with us forever.

Three months after Royal came to live with us, his baby sister was born. She is an angel. I can't even describe what it's like to be in her presence. Five pounds and two ounces of laughter and sass rang our doorbell that September day. She is pure joy contained in a tiny human body. She has the spiritual gift of hugs. They love us and love each other fiercely. She sings happy birthday to Royal every morning just because he woke up and asked for pancakes. They are best friends and will have such a special bond for the rest of their lives - once they stop hitting each other in the face of course.

Geez! I'm pretty sure we're more tired of Time Out than they are.

In the span of time before their parents lost their rights, we experienced the immense joy of watching them grow while we felt the fear of still possibly losing them. The heart-pounding realization would hit us at random times reminding us the babies we were holding might not be ours forever. Yet it is still hard to see people separated from their children, no matter their situation or decision-making paradigm. We were praying that the kids would be ours while at the same time praying for their bio parents' redemption and restoration. It was the hardest and most dissonant prayer we've ever prayed. These were prayers that dug deep wells in our souls. Wells that only God could fill with living water.

We saw the grief in their bio mom's eyes when she relinquished her rights to them. We watched the scene unfold as their father's rights were terminated in a dramatic and intense court hearing. We took them to the last visit where they would say goodbye. I remember not knowing how to feel when their mom kissed Sissy for the last time. I remember the look on her face. I can never forget it.

After two years of being their foster parents, we stood before the judge and affirmed our love, commitment, and covenant to raise these precious children as our own. We adopted them together on July 26th, 2018. And then Royal threw a teddy bear at the judge's face. Bro.

In our experiences of fostering and adoption, we learned that each day is an opportunity to love the children that have been placed in our home. The kids win because they've been loved. We win because we've given love. The state of Texas (in our case) wins because we stepped up to care for her children in need. The kingdom of God wins because children from hard places are being cared for. The gospel wins because every time we say yes to a child we are telling them and the world that God is willing to go to any length to express his love.

After eleven years of marriage our family is not at all what Emily and I innocently imagined on that first date.

It's unimaginably better.

David & Emily Gentiles
Foster and Adoptive Parents

A PURE AND UNDEFILED REFLECTION

–

Caring for vulnerable children and families is one of the purest and most undefiled demonstrations of the gospel this world will ever see.

PRAY

—

As you gather the group together, begin with prayer. Each group member should have the opportunity to share any particular requests they would like the group to pray for. Use this time as an opportunity to encourage one another and focus your hearts and minds on what God may have in store during your time together.

CONNECT

—

Spend the next 5-10 minutes connecting as a group. Catch up on what's going on in each other's lives.

- *How has your week been?*
- *Did anything out of the ordinary or particularly interesting happen?*
- *Is anything coming up for you between now and the next group meeting that you want group members to know?*

In Session 2, we learned about the multi-generational scope of the gospel in our lives – how it breaks pasts cycles, forms new present realities and alters the future trajectory of our lives forever. In this session, we will explore how the gospel of our redemption through Jesus is vividly and tangibly seen through our care of the most vulnerable around us.

There's a variety of ways God allows us to "see" Him throughout our lives. To begin this session, share with the group different ways you "see" God in your daily life.

- *What experiences, interactions and encounters do you find focus your mind and heart on Him the most?*

- *What draws your heart into worship of Him?*

- *What in your life right now is teaching you the most about the character and nature of who God is?*

GROW

—

James 1:27

Let's briefly revisit our discussion on James 1:27 from Session 1. Recall that we discussed the "descriptive" nature of what James is saying, and paraphrased his intent with the following synopsis: **One of the purest and most undefiled outward demonstrations of the gospel which is inwardly true in us is to see hard places and broken people and move towards them, not away from them.** Why? Because this is exactly what Jesus has done for us!

THREE PURE AND UNDEFILED REFLECTIONS OF THE GOSPEL

In light of that, let's explore three tangible ways we see the gospel demonstrated through our care of the vulnerable and orphaned. (Note: This list is not exhaustive, just representative of truths we'll all encounter along our journey, wherever it might lead us.)

1) Caring for the vulnerable demands we step towards broken stories just as Jesus stepped into ours.

READ:

Matthew 1:23 —

> *"Behold, the virgin shall conceive and bear a son, and they shall call his name Immanuel" (which means, God with us).*

Philippians 2:5-8 —

> *Have this mind among yourselves, which is yours in Christ Jesus, who, though he was in the form of God, did not count equality with God a thing to be grasped, but emptied himself, by taking the form of a servant, being born in the likeness of men. And being found in human form, he humbled himself by becoming obedient to the point of death, even death on a cross.*

This is what we celebrate at Christmas, right? (His incarnation - see Session 2) That God said, *"I see you where you are, and I'm coming after you!"* He took the form of a servant and entered into our broken story in order to walk with us in it and ultimately redeem us from it.

The gospel of Jesus Christ means our families and churches ought to be at the forefront of the adoption of orphans close to home and around the world.

– Russell Moore

Jesus pulled us out of a broken story by first humbly and willingly being pulled into it. He joyfully accepted any and all implications that would come down on Him for our sake. In a similar way, as we engage in the care of the vulnerable and orphaned in this world, we must be willing to love them as Jesus has loved us by engaging them where they are, embracing the brokenness of where they come from and allowing their plight to change us, no matter the implications.

Caring for the vulnerable is just as much about pulling a child out of a broken story as it is about you being pulled into one. In foster care, it could mean hard court hearings, navigating through an imperfect state-run child welfare system, difficult meetings with biological parents, case workers and lawyers and having your heart broken and world shattered by the difficult contexts which the child you are now caring for comes from. In adoption, it could mean engaging with a confused young lady going through an unexpected and unwanted pregnancy. It could mean persevering through the bureaucracy of overseas governments and officials overseeing institutional care in their country. It could mean developing long-term relationships with the biological family after adoption and navigating the often difficult relational roads that come along with that. It could even mean engaging in the life of a struggling family and doing whatever it takes to help them become whole and healthy so their family can stay together. No foster care. No adoption. Just family restoration.

Caring for the vulnerable is a beautiful thing, but it certainly is not a fairy tale. You will love more passionately, hurt more deeply, grieve more bitterly and celebrate more joyously throughout the process of caring for vulnerable children than you ever thought imaginable. This is the hard reality of where this journey begins, where it takes you, what it requires of you and how it will break you. We must be willing to walk down this path for their sake. As we do, our loving embrace of their brokenness paints a vivid picture of how Jesus embraced ours.

Your friends might look at you like you're crazy. Your family might look at you like you're crazy. Your coworkers and neighbors might look at you like you're crazy. You'll even look at yourself sometimes and think, "I'm crazy!" And you're right - it's crazy that Jesus would do this for us, and crazy that He gives us the privilege to do it for others!

2) Caring for the vulnerable requires that we stand for justice in a deeply spiritual battle just as Jesus stood for us.

READ:

1 Timothy 2:5-6 —

> *For there is one God, and there is one mediator between God and men, the man Christ Jesus, who gave himself as a ransom for all, which is the testimony given at the proper time.*

1 John 2:1-2 —

> *My little children, I am writing these things to you so that you may not sin. But if anyone does sin, we have an advocate with the Father, Jesus Christ the righteous. He is the propitiation for our sins, and not for ours only but also for the sins of the whole world.*

The Bible describes Jesus as our "advocate" and "mediator," the One who testified before God on our behalf. He stood in the gap for us, destroying the rights of the enemy over our lives and assuming those rights upon Himself. He took full ownership of us and accepted the cost of His own life He would have to pay so that justice could be brought about in our lives.

In a similar way, our call is to fight for justice on behalf of the marginalized and vulnerable – to stand for them, advocate for them and assume responsibility for them. **The gospel expects, albeit demands, that we be willing to stand for them where Jesus has stood for us**, seeking justice in the midst of their brokenness.

READ:

Ephesians 6:12 —

> *For we do not wrestle against flesh and blood, but against the rulers, against the authorities, against the cosmic powers over this present darkness, against the spiritual forces of evil in the heavenly places.*

John 10:10 —

> *The thief comes only to steal and kill and destroy. I came that they may have life and have it abundantly.*

The Bible says that in our fight for good over evil, we do not wrestle against any one person or group of people, but rather we fight against spiritual powers and authorities of darkness. In the end, the war we fight is against a spiritual enemy who wants to steal, kill and destroy families.

In our standing for a child, we do not stand against their biological families, no matter the abuse, neglect or oppression they may be guilty of committing (especially in foster care situations). In many cases, it is heinous and our natural tendencies will be anger and bitterness towards them. However, in the end, as we stand for these kids, we do not stand against their parents but against the enemy who celebrates devastation and works towards injustice in their lives. We don't fight against people, or a broken system, but against powers and forces and darkness and evil and injustice. These are the true villians in all of this. We all - us as foster or adoptive families, these kids and the families they come from are actually fighitng the same enemy - and it's not each other.

The real enemy in all of this is not a biological mom or dad, an agency or a system, but Satan who seeks to steal, kill and destroy families. It follows then since Satan is the real enemy, Jesus can be the only true hero. We must stand where He would stand on behalf of what He would stand for, not so we are seen as heroic but so He is seen as the ultimate hero in the battle for what is good and right and just. The gospel crucifies our "hero complex" and need to be seen, and points to Jesus as the true hero in all of this.

3) Caring for the vulnerable demands we lay down our lives for others just as Jesus laid down His life for us.

READ:

2 Corinthians 5:21 —

> *For our sake he made him to be sin who knew no sin, so that in him we might become the righteousness of God.*

2 Corinthians 8:9 —

> *For you know the grace of our Lord Jesus Christ, that*
> *though he was rich, yet for your sake he became poor, so*
> *that you by his poverty might become rich.*

The gospel is the story of a "great exchange" – God's righteousness for our unrighteousness, His holiness for our sin, the fullness of His glory for our emptiness. He suffered and died so that we could live.

And like our Savior, who poured out His life and blood so we have reason to rejoice, we were made to lay down our lives and give until it hurts. We are most alive when we are loving and actively giving of ourselves because we were made to do these things.

– Francis Chan

Jesus laid down the infinite value of His own life so that we might know the immeasurable worth of being fully loved by Him. In a similar way, our call to care for the marginalized and orphaned is ultimately the call to accept the costs we may incur as worth it for the gain a child may receive through our love for them. This is nothing less than what Jesus has done for us, so we are compelled to do it for them. We must always keep this perspective, because when it gets hard and we begin to question whether or not the cost is worth it, it is being reminded of the gospel and the lengths Jesus went to call us His own that will carry us and sustain us through.

This journey will at times stretch the limits of who we are and what we are capable of. It will take us places emotionally, spiritually and even physically we never imagined. It will cost us, but in the end the value of the life of a child far exceeds the value of anything lesser we may have to lose in order to love that child.

Here's a short list of "costs" many can anticipate incurring in the call to care to foster, adopt or support families. *As a group, discuss some of these and see if you can think of any others:*

- *Money*
- *Comfort*
- *The picture of the "ideal family"*
- *Your schedule*
- *Your car or house may be too small with an extra kid*
- _____
- _____
- _____
- _____
- _____
- _____

Gospel-Centered vs. Family-Centered Thinking

Our care of vulnerable children must be gospel-centered in scope, otherwise the tendency to be family-centered will dominate our motivations. To be gospel-centered means to always keep at the forefront of our thinking the belief that it is better to give than to receive, and that true service of others almost always involves true sacrifice of self.

Family-Centered	**Gospel-Centered**
♦ *Family growth mechanism*	♦ *Family giving mechanism*
♦ *Begins with our family's wants*	♦ *Begins with a child's needs*
♦ *What a child can offer us*	♦ *What we can offer a child*

If you were to take an honest evaluation of your heart today, where would you fall on this spectrum?

What steps can you take to increasingly move yourself towards a giving, gospel-centered posture?

Foster care and adoption are first family-giving mechanisms before they are family-growth mechanisms. They're not about getting a child for our family but rather giving our family for a child — and willingly embracing the implications that come along with that. That's not to say that a family can't grow through adoption — it obviously does — or that a family doesn't receive endless amounts of blessings and joy through foster care — it no doubt can. It is to say, however, that our first call is to give, not receive — to recognize that true service of others almost always involves true sacrifice of self. Only the gospel can produce that posture.

As a group, spend a few minutes discussing why it is important to distinguish between a family-centered approach and a gospel-centered one.

DISCUSS

As you close your time together, spend 5-10 minutes processing the things you have learned and discussed. This is an especially important opportunity to share thoughts, feelings, questions, concerns or any resolutions you have made in response to your study.

- *What truth or idea stood out to you most in this session? Why?*

- *Why is it so important for us to understand the theology of the gospel as it pertains to our care of orphans?*

- *What concerns or fears do you have about the "costs" associated in caring for the marginalized, neglected, abused and orphaned? What specifically, if anything, comes to your mind immediately when we talk about the things you must be willing to "lose" in order for a child to gain?*

REFLECT

As you reflect on the truths of this session and consider the personal implications for your own life, spend some time writing and processing through the following three concepts:

1. *Write about some unique aspects of the gospel that stood out to you most in this session.*

2. *Write a letter to your family (maybe any current children you have, a spouse that is unsure about the calling to foster or adopt, or any extended family that may be a part of helping support you as you care for children) explaining why you believe God is calling you to "give your family" (including them) to a child and what that could mean for everyone involved.*

3. *Write out a prayer to God, asking Him for the strength to always keep "giving" as your primary motivation and perspective. Ask Him for courage to take the next steps in the process of caring for vulnerable and orphaned children and to willingly accept the costs as worth it for the gain a child may receive.*

REFLECTIVE WRITING

_____

_____

_____

_____

_____

_____

_____

_____

_____

_____

_____

_____

_____

_____

_____

_____

_____

_____

_____

_____

ADDITIONAL SCRIPTURE TO USE IN PRAYER:

John 3:16; John 10:10; 2 Corinthians 1:3–5; Colossians 1:13; Psalm 82:3; Romans 8:26–28

HEAD: *What biblical truth did you learn from this?*

_____

_____

HEART: *What do the ideas we are discussing make you think and feel?*

_____

_____

HANDS: *What are you going to do in response to what we have learned?*

_____

_____

–

ON THE
OTHER SIDE

–

Jessica and Philip Pattison
Foster and Adoptive Parents
www.fosterthebay.org

The world of foster care can feel like a terrifying, turbulent ocean -- the type of waters that one only desires to know from a distance. However, like the first disciples of Jesus, we are called to venture out into deeper, unknown waters. On our own personal journey as foster parents, my husband and I have definitely been led to that stormy place.

Our first placement was a beautiful baby girl. I will refer to her here as "Sissa" (her nickname). When we were matched with Sissa, we were told of the high probability that she would return to her birth parents. During the beginning months with her, my heart was so very confused. It would be dishonest of me if I said that I didn't have a hope to be her forever mommy. However, her parents did not resemble the typical story I had heard about with so many other little ones. They showed up for every visit, waited eagerly for her, and did everything that was asked of them. A couple months into us caring for her, her parents had one of their first hearings which would determine whether or not the county was justified in removing their child from their home. The ruling was not in their favor, and they were not granted permission to take her home that day. They did, however, have a visit scheduled for that evening.

That night when I drove to the county building where I would drop off Sissa for her visit, I didn't have our other three children with me. I was alone. In that moment, I felt a nudge from the Holy Spirit to drop Sissa off in a very different way than I had previously done. Often I would drop her off in a location at the main building that would allow me to stay in the car with the kids, and the visitation social worker would come to get her. Doing it this way meant that there is no interaction with the birth parents. It makes it a lot easier when you have a bunch of little kids in the car. No need to unbuckle, corral, and buckle back into the car. It also doesn't allow for lengthy conversations with the birth parents, which was a welcomed buffer for my fearful heart.

So when I sensed the Spirit prompting me to walk Sissa in on such a heavy day, you could say I was more than a little nervous. Not only was I motivated to ask them about their court hearing while waiting for the visitation social worker, but I felt the push to pray with them. I asked them if they would be open to me praying with them after they had responded about the day's events. They were open to it, so we huddled in the lobby of the DFCS (Department of Family and Children's Services), which just seemed super crazy to me! In our prayer, I asked God that we would be united and on the same team, that we would all give Sissa the best possible life that we could, and above all always keep her best interests in mind.

My hope of being her forever mommy would quickly fade into the distance. Walls came down between us, walls that had once given me a false sense of comfort but had ultimately never seemed to cast out the fear in my heart. The fear that it had to be "biological parents versus foster parents" was removed that day; now, we were united in our love for this precious little one. That day, God asked me to step into the mess and the pain a little further. It was extremely difficult to be obedient, but through that obedience God poured out a healing balm on our hearts that became the bond of love between our two families.

Sissa is now happily reunited with her family. Her time with us and on this fostering journey continues to challenge me and the walls of safety I often choose to hide behind. I sometimes think that those on the other side of our walls may not understand that we are cowering in fear of the unknown. The walls we put up can offend, oppress, and keep us from the very thing we all really desire: love. But there is something very good to be found on the other side of the walls we build up. It is often messy, but with Christ, bridges can be built to connect us and establish a greater empathy in us for one another. Whether you have walls or perhaps unchartered waters in front of you, I encourage you to take a leap forward because there is something so much sweeter than safety to be had on the other side of your fears.

Jessica and Philip Pattison
Foster and Adoptive Parents
www.fosterthebay.org

—

THE OTHER SIDE OF THE STORY

—

God loves people enough to engage them where they are and loves them too much to allow them to stay there.

PRAY

—

As you gather the group together, begin with prayer. Each group member should have the opportunity to share any particular requests they would like the group to pray for. Use this time as an opportunity to encourage one another and focus your hearts and minds on what God may have in store during your time together.

CONNECT

—

Spend the next 5-10 minutes connecting as a group. Catch up on what's going on in each other's lives.

- *How has your week been?*
- *Did anything out of the ordinary or particularly interesting happen?*
- *Is anything coming up for you between now and the next group meeting that you want group members to know?*

In Session 3, we looked at specific ways the gospel can vividly be displayed and tangibly demonstrated through care of the vulnerable. During this session, we will discuss the importance of engaging families in their circumstances to prevent children from needing to be removed from their care.

As you begin this session, share your answers to the following questions with the group:

- *Can you describe a time in your life when God protected you from something by preventing what was necessary to get you there from ever even happening?*

◆　*How did you feel at the time? What have you learned as a result of looking back on that time with a different perspective?*

GROW

—

When God Prevents, God Protects

God intercedes on behalf of people. His character always bends Him towards the helpless and hurting, not away from them. His heart always compels Him to act for their good, never their harm. Consistently throughout Scripture, we see God stepping into people's circumstances, not simply to prevent them from engaging in certain behaviors but ultimately to protect them from the devastating consequences that those behaviors will bring about in their lives. His restrictions are always redemptive in purpose.

Let's look at a couple of examples of this in Scripture:

The Story of Jonah

Jonah was called by God to go to an evil city called Nineveh and preach repentance there. Instead, Jonah chose to go against the purpose of God and began traveling in the opposite direction towards a town called Tarshish. His journey would get a little precarious at times, and his attempts to run from God would ultimately end unsuccessfully.

Let's see why:

READ:

Jonah 1:4-16 —

> The Lord hurled a great wind upon the sea, and there
> was a mighty tempest on the sea, so that the ship
> threatened to break up. Then the mariners were afraid,
> and each cried out to his god. And they hurled the cargo
> that was in the ship into the sea to lighten it for them.
> But Jonah had gone down into the inner part of the ship
> and had lain down and was fast asleep. So the captain
> came and said to him, "What do you mean, you sleeper?
> Arise, call out to your god! Perhaps the god will give a
> thought to us, that we may not perish."
>
> They said to one another, "Come, let us cast lots, that
> we may know on whose account this evil has come upon
> us." So they cast lots, and the lot fell on Jonah. Then they
> said to him, "Tell us on whose account this evil has come
> upon us. What is your occupation? And where do you
> come from? What is your country? And of what people
> are you?" And he said to them, "I am a Hebrew, and I
> fear the Lord, the God of heaven, who made the sea and
> the dry land." Then the men were exceedingly afraid and
> said to him, "What is this that you have done!" For the
> men knew that he was fleeing from the presence of the
> Lord, because he had told them.
>
> Then they said to him, "What shall we do to you, that the
> sea may quiet down for us?" For the sea grew more and
> more tempestuous. He said to them, "Pick me up and
> hurl me into the sea; then the sea will quiet down for you,

for I know it is because of me that this great tempest has come upon you." Nevertheless, the men rowed hard1 to get back to dry land, but they could not, for the sea grew more and more tempestuous against them. Therefore they called out to the Lord, "O Lord, let us not perish for this man's life, and lay not on us innocent blood, for you, O Lord, have done as it pleased you." So they picked up Jonah and hurled him into the sea, and the sea ceased from its raging. Then the men feared the Lord exceedingly, and they offered a sacrifice to the Lord and made vows.

What about the sailors' reaction to the storm and Jonah's response to them stands out to you most in this passage?

Jonah is running from God. He's in self-destruct mode. When we read the story through this lens how should we view the storm? Is it Jonah's punishment or is it Jonah's rescue?

Explain how this storm, and Jonah subsequently being thrown overboard, can be viewed as God's merciful intervention in his life. What did it prevent him from doing? How did it protect him from the consequences of doing it?

READ:

Jonah 1:17 —

And the Lord appointed a great fish to swallow up Jonah. And Jonah was in the belly of the fish three days and three nights.

79

Jonah 2:1, 10 —

> *Then Jonah prayed to the Lord his God from the belly of the fish ... and the Lord spoke to the fish, and it vomited Jonah out upon the dry land.*

God had already sent a storm to stop Jonah from arriving at Tarshish. How do we see Him continue to intervene in this passage?

We often think of the whale as punishment, and it, of course, is an uncomfortable place that Jonah found himself due to his disobedience. As uncomfortable as it may be, how can the belly of the whale be seen as the merciful intervention of God on behalf of Jonah?

Consider where Jonah was and what was about to happen to him before the whale swallowed him up. What did it prevent from occurring? How does this redefine or broaden our understanding of what God's mercy looks like, how it works and how it may sometimes feel in our lives?

The story of Jonah shows that God's heart is to mercifully intervene in the lives of those who are in self-destruct mode. His heart is to prevent us from the consequences of certain behaviors in order to protect us from the brokenness, loss, shame and despair those behaviors will ultimately lead to. His mercy is necessary no matter how uncomfortable it may be at the time.

The Story of the Woman at the Well

This unnamed woman, known most commonly as "the woman at the well," was a poor woman from Samaria who had quite a reputation. She had been married five times and was now living in sin with a man who wasn't her husband. On what seemed to be just another day of tasks of which included fetching water from a nearby well, she would meet Jesus and never be the same.

READ:

John 4:7-18 —

> *A woman from Samaria came to draw water. Jesus said to her, "Give me a drink." (For his disciples had gone away into the city to buy food.) The Samaritan woman said to him, "How is it that you, a Jew, ask for a drink from me, a woman of Samaria?" (For Jews have no dealings with Samaritans.) Jesus answered her, "If you knew the gift of God, and who it is that is saying to you, 'Give me a drink,' you would have asked him, and he would have given you living water." The woman said to him, "Sir, you have nothing to draw water with, and the well is deep. Where do you get that living water? Are you greater than our father Jacob? He gave us the well and drank from it himself, as did his sons and his livestock." Jesus said to her, "Everyone who drinks of this water will be thirsty again, but whoever drinks of the water that I will give him will never be thirsty again. The water that I will give him will become in him a spring of water welling up to eternal life." The woman said to him, "Sir, give me this water, so that I will not be thirsty or have to come here to draw water."*

> *Jesus said to her, "Go, call your husband, and come here."*
> *The woman answered him, "I have no husband." Jesus said*
> *to her, "You are right in saying, 'I have no husband'; for you*
> *have had five husbands, and the one you now have is not*
> *your husband. What you have said is true.".*

This Samaritan woman is going about her daily business, all while hiding the dark secrets of her sordid and broken life. She asks Jesus for spiritual nourishment. What stands out to you about His response?

Jesus presses on the deepest parts of her shame, not to hurt her, but to heal her. How does His approach with her demonstrate love and mercy? How does it set her free from the consequences of continuing in her destructive behavior?

READ:

John 4:25-30 —

> *The woman said to him, "I know that Messiah is coming*
> *(he who is called Christ). When he comes, he will tell us all*
> *things." Jesus said to her, "I who speak to you am he."*

> *Just then his disciples came back. They marveled that he*
> *was talking with a woman, but no one said, "What do you*
> *seek?" or, "Why are you talking with her?" So the woman*
> *left her water jar and went away into town and said to the*
> *people, "Come, see a man who told me all that I ever did.*
> *Can this be the Christ?" They went out of the town and*
> *were coming to him.*

John 4:39-42 —

> *Many Samaritans from that town believed in him because of the woman's testimony, "He told me all that I ever did." So when the Samaritans came to him, they asked him to stay with them, and he stayed there two days. And many more believed because of his word. They said to the woman, "It is no longer because of what you said that we believe, for we have heard for ourselves, and we know that this is indeed the Savior of the world."*

What is her response to Jesus? Is she angry at Him for "meddling in her business"? Is she offended that He would step into her situation, expose it for what it was and then offer His hand as a solution?

What do we learn about God's intervention into people's lives who are in self-destruct mode through this story? What kind of impact did it have on her life and the lives of those around her?

The story of The Woman at the Well shows that Jesus came to save the sick, set the captive free and heal the hurting. He loves people enough to engage them where they are and loves them too much to allow them to stay there. He engages people in their darkest places in order to bring them into the light. He presses where it hurts at times, not to cause harm but to heal, bring freedom and draw them into greater depths of intimacy with Himself.

The Two Sides Of the Same Story

The goal in caring for kids from hard places is always safe permanence – providing children the opportunity to grow up in a loving, supportive and nurturing family environment. This is the singular purpose for which all of our efforts are exclusively aimed. However, the means by which that one purpose are accomplished are two-fold:

1. *Through restoration of and/or reunification with the family of origin.*
2. *Through adoption into a new forever family.*

Both accomplish the goal of a child being raised in a permanent family structure – one involves a child from one family entering into another family, the other involves preventing a child from being permanently removed from their family through alternative forms of care.

One is reactive in nature, especially in foster care situations where a child may experience abuse or neglect and is in need of someone stepping in to protect them. Often times, the severity of circumstances requires swift and immediate measures to protect the rights of the vulnerable. This is a good and just solution to a very real problem and a pure reflection of the heart of God to intercede on behalf of the helpless and hopeless.

The other is proactive in nature, responding to the struggles of families and interceding with alternative forms of care — counseling, mentoring and rehabilitation efforts — to help keep families together. This too is right and honorable and a clear reflection of the heart of God to bring healing to what is broken and hope to what otherwise may have led to devastating consequences.

Both are necessary and both are essential.

Orphan care is bigger than just adopting children who have no families, it's also the responsibility we have, whenever possible, to do whatever is necessary to prevent kids from ever becoming orphans.

Consider this hypothetical, but very realistic story of a little boy we will call Johnny.

Johnny was born into a difficult environment. His father is in prison and his mother has struggled with drug addictions most of her adult life. She was using while pregnant with him, requiring state child welfare services to intervene after his birth in the hospital. Johnny was immediately removed from her care and placed in a local foster home. While this foster family was honored to care for Johnny, they were also devastated over the fact that it was brokenness and struggle that led him to them.

As the weeks and months of court hearings and parent visitations transpired, Johnny's foster parents learned more and more of his mother's story – she too had grown up in a home riddled with drug addiction and abuse. Those past generational patterns of brokenness evolved into her life and the effects were now perpetuating themselves into the life of her son. She was devastated over this and desperately needed help to get out from underneath the demons in her life that had been passed down to her and she was now passing down to him.

Johnny's foster parents began to understand that their involvement in his life was bigger than just him. They had stepped foot into the middle of generational cycles of brokenness and been given the opportunity to bring hope and healing – not just to a little boy, but to the family of that little boy as well.

In this hypothetical story of Johnny and his parents, we are reminded that the story of a struggling family and cycles of generational brokenness often precede our involvement in that child's life. Our care of vulnerable children is crucial, but so is our fuller awareness of the contexts from which they come.

Question: What is your current posture towards biological families? Fear? Anger? Uncertainty? Compassion?

Why is Prevention So Important?

It's impossible to get away from the fact that God loves us enough to mercifully intervene in our lives – to both prevent us from engaging in destructive behavior and protect us from the consequences of those behaviors. We see that all throughout scripture. Not only does He love us enough to engage us where we are, as uncomfortable as it may be at times, He also loves us too much to allow us to stay there.

The reality of His proactive involvement in our lives in this capacity then begs the question of us:

How are we proactively, mercifully and lovingly interceding into the lives of broken and struggling families, as uncomfortable and hard as it may be at times, to bring hope and healing to an otherwise tragic situation?

This, too, is orphan care – working to prevent the need for more orphans to be cared for.

There are some pretty clear solutions that can be offered when it comes to responding to a child who is in need, whether it be offer a safe, temporary home for them, legally foster them or even provide permanence for them through adoption. However, the solutions are not so clearly defined when it comes to proactively engaging families in order to prevent children from being removed from them.

At a minimum, our hope in this session is to expose both sides of the same story and to bring awareness to the holistic picture of all that transpires in cases of child and family welfare. Perhaps, as you prayerfully discern where God is leading you to get involved, you will be drawn not only to the children but to the noble task of interceding on behalf of those children's families to help keep them together. We encourage you to to talk to your church or research local organizations to explore potential opportunities to do just that.

DISCUSS

As you close your time together, spend 5-10 minutes processing the things you have learned and discussed. This is an especially important opportunity to share thoughts, feelings, questions, concerns or any resolutions you have made in response to your study.

- *What truth or idea stood out to you most in this session? Why?*

- *Why is it important for us to understand both sides of the orphan care issue?*

- *What do the truths and ideas discussed in the session make you think about your own calling to care for the vulnerable kids and families?*

REFLECT

As you reflect on the truths of this session and consider the personal implications for your own life, spend some time writing and praying through the following three questions:

1. *What is your current posture and attitude towards the biological families of children who are in need of help? How can you ask God to increase your capacity to have compassion not just on the child, but on the family as well?*

2. *Having been exposed to "the other side of the story," what questions, fears or concerns do you have about what that might mean for you as you seek to live out the heart of God by interceding on behalf of the vulnerable and struggling?*

3. *Consider again the "parameters" you have defined for how you want to engage in this. Are you willing to let God expand those and have you step into areas of involvement you were not necessarily preparing yourself for? Why? Why not?*

REFLECTIVE WRITING

_____

_____

_____

_____

_____

_____

_____

_____

_____

_____

_____

_____

_____

_____

_____

_____

_____

_____

_____

_____

ADDITIONAL SCRIPTURE TO USE IN PRAYER:

Matthew 10:26–31; Hebrews 4:12–13; 2 Corinthians 5:17;
Galatians 6:1; 1 Samuel 16:7; Romans 12:1–2

 HEAD: *What biblical truth did you learn from this?*

_____

_____

 HEART: *What do the ideas we are discussing make you think and feel?*

_____

_____

 HANDS: *What are you going to do in response to what we have learned?*

_____

_____

–

EMBRACING THE UNKNOWNS

–

Ade and Jenni Olowo

Foster and Adoptive Parents

I like to be in control. If I had my choice my days would be filled with only things I can predict, plan, and organize. Everything I had heard about foster care seemed like the opposite of that. I sat in our orientation meeting asking endless questions, clearly trying to predict the future outcome of a foster care placement that didn't even exist yet. The Director of our agency chuckled at me a little and couldn't resist making a joke about how obviously I was someone who does not like spontaneity and unknowns.

Preparing for foster care fit into my neat little box of self-preservation. We knew we would open to a 0-24 months old, boy or girl, so I was able to get every item one can imagine on a registry that covered that entire range. I even put together a box of clothing and diapers that has sizes spanning the age range and both genders so we would be totally prepared. We bought a crib that would work for a newborn, or work for a toddler. It was easy to talk about foster care with people who asked questions because it was seeming to follow a fairly predictable path.

The day we got "the call" asking us to be a family to a 22-month-old girl changed our lives forever. When I heard the basic details of her case it seemed undeniable that this placement would lead to adoption. I almost felt a sense of relief that we were given an unusual case, one that didn't involve the normal elements of the story, which would surely be easier.

Little did we know that her case would be the opposite of predictable. We had no idea that summer day when she arrived that her case would go 3 days shy of a jury trial with more days in court than we were prepared for. Before foster care I had never spoken to an attorney. Before foster care I had never laid eyes on legal documentation for a judge. Before foster care I had no idea where the office of the Department of Family and Protective Services was in my city. Before foster care I didn't know the way our daughter's biological family would touch the deepest places of our lives. Before foster care I had not truly known, in the depths of my soul, the unchanging nature of God the Father.

A choice we as a family had to make was how we would respond to God throughout the unknowns. Would we be able to confidently stand and say He is good no matter what the outcome? This became a daily pleading with the Lord.

The safe walls I had put around my comfortable life quickly crumbled as this first foster care placement became an unpredictable nightmare. We heard the phrase, "in all my years of being involved in CPS cases I've never seen anything like this happen" more times than we like to admit from many of the key players involved. Each birthday, holiday, special event became a giant question mark. Would this be the first and only time we get to celebrate as a family?

It would be easy in these moments to put up protective walls.

Foster care was turning out to be a more raw and vulnerable process than I could have ever imagined. As first-time parents my husband and I knew that if our foster daughter could be safely reunified to family, we would no longer be parents in reality, only in our hearts. Keeping ourselves emotionally distant from our daughter would seem like the safest option. Foster care changed us because we knew, beyond the shadow of a doubt, that we would have to give her our all for this thing to really "work", even it meant we could not control the outcomes.

We spent countless nights discussing, "what will we do if she leaves?" "How will we survive this?" I have distinct memories of Christmastime that first year sitting on the couch at midnight crying so hard I could hardly breath. In the depths of my soul I felt Jesus drawing me to Himself. I poured over the Psalms, praising and lamenting, searching for promises from God. The hardest part of foster care is that as a foster parent we are largely not in control. There is very little you can do to change the outcome in most cases. What I could control, however, was doing my best during the time we had with her – no matter how long or short – to make a difference in the life of one little girl who really needed a Mommy and Daddy that were safe and stable.

I often asked myself if I would rather skip out on all the pain I was experiencing over the unknowns, wishing I had never become a foster parent. Each time that thought came to mind it was met with a resounding, "No!" I wouldn't trade a moment of my pain for not knowing this little girl. I was watching her transform before my eyes from a scared helpless child, to a confident and bold little girl. Her healing and redemption made it worth it, even if I was only in her life for a season.

Foster care has taught me that I am a lot stronger than I thought. My husband is a lot stronger than he thought. The little girl who made us parents is far braver than she knows. Foster care threatened on many occasions to break us emotionally, physically, and spiritually because of the unknowns and lack of control, but keeping our eyes firmly fixed on the One who can be a firm foundation helped us take one step at a time and see this first foster care journey through to completion. The beautiful ways Jesus provided for us and held us up astound us. We know Jesus today in new and unique ways because of the foster care journey. In that regard, the pain and struggle and beauty and triumph have all been a gift – the mercy of God to draw us deeper into Himself.

Today, 6 months post adoption of the little girl who stole our hearts, we hold in our arms a 3-month-old baby boy with a completely new and different story. We are a little more seasoned, expectations of foster care itself are a little clearer, but our need for Jesus to light our path through foster care is the same. We don't know if he will need to be adopted or if he will get to go back home. The one thing I can be very sure of is that at the end of this new journey we will not be the same people. We will be a little stronger, a little more raw, and we will know Jesus in new and deeper ways than ever before.

This is foster care.

Ade and Jenni Olowo
Foster and Adoptive Parents

—

SHRINKING THE PROBLEM

—

You may not be able to change the world for everyone, but you can change the world of someone.

PRAY

—

As you gather the group together, begin with prayer. Each group member should have the opportunity to share any particular requests they would like the group to pray for. Use this time as an opportunity to encourage one another and focus your hearts and minds on what God may have in store during your time together.

CONNECT

—

Spend the next 5-10 minutes connecting as a group. Catch up on what's going on in each other's lives.

- *How has your week been?*
- *Did anything out of the ordinary or particularly interesting happen?*
- *Is anything coming up for you between now and the next group meeting that you want group members to know?*

In Session 4, we looked at "the other side of the story" and were exposed to the reality of the contexts many vulnerable children come from. In this session, we will spend time looking at some current statistics that will help give us a picture of what the global and domestic crisis looks like. We'll see that the need is overwhelming, but our opportunity to make a difference is very real. Jesus is changing the world one person at a time, and so can we.

As you begin this session, share your answers to the following questions with the group:

- *Can you describe a time in your life when someone went out of their way to serve you, make you feel special or love you in ways that you very specifically needed at the time?*

- *How did that make you feel? Looking back on it now, how has it helped shape the person that you are today?*

GROW

—

Changing the World of One

The Kingdom of God redefines and reorients most of what the world says is valuable and worth giving our lives over to. Jesus is constantly inverting the order of things and setting into a motion a new and better way of living. He says the first will be last and the last will be first (Matthew 20:16), if you want to find your life you must first lose it (Luke 9:24) and the least likely among you usually ends up being the greatest (Luke 9:48). His message consistently represented a reversal of the world's values.

This theme carries through into some very familiar parables Jesus uses to illustrate the lengths to which He would go in order to save just one soul.

READ:

Luke 15:1-32 —

> *Now the tax collectors and sinners were all drawing near to hear him. And the Pharisees and the scribes grumbled, saying, "This man receives sinners and eats with them."*

So he told them this parable: "What man of you, having a hundred sheep, if he has lost one of them, does not leave the ninety-nine in the open country, and go after the one that is lost, until he finds it? And when he has found it, he lays it on his shoulders, rejoicing. And when he comes home, he calls together his friends and his neighbors, saying to them, 'Rejoice with me, for I have found my sheep that was lost.' Just so, I tell you, there will be more joy in heaven over one sinner who repents than over ninety-nine righteous persons who need no repentance.

"Or what woman, having ten silver coins, if she loses one coin, does not light a lamp and sweep the house and seek diligently until she finds it? And when she has found it, she calls together her friends and neighbors, saying, 'Rejoice with me, for I have found the coin that I had lost.' Just so, I tell you, there is joy before the angels of God over one sinner who repents."

And he said, "There was a man who had two sons. And the younger of them said to his father, 'Father, give me the share of property that is coming to me.' And he divided his property between them. Not many days later, the younger son gathered all he had and took a journey into a far country, and there he squandered his property in reckless living. And when he had spent everything, a severe famine arose in that country, and he began to be in need. So he went and hired himself out to one of the citizens of that country, who sent him into his fields to feed pigs. And he was longing to be fed with the pods that the pigs ate, and no one gave him anything.

"But when he came to himself, he said, 'How many of my father's hired servants have more than enough bread, but I perish here with hunger! I will arise and go to my father, and I will say to him, "Father, I have sinned against heaven and before you. I am no longer worthy to be called your son. Treat me as one of your hired servants."' And he arose and came to his father. But while he was still a long way off, his father saw him and felt compassion, and ran and embraced him and kissed him. And the son said to him, 'Father, I have sinned against heaven and before you. I am no longer worthy to be called your son.' But the father said to his servants, 'Bring quickly the best robe, and put it on him, and put a ring on his hand, and shoes on his feet. And bring the fattened calf and kill it, and let us eat and celebrate. For this my son was dead, and is alive again; he was lost, and is found.' And they began to celebrate.

"Now his older son was in the field, and as he came and drew near to the house, he heard music and dancing. And he called one of the servants and asked what these things meant. And he said to him, 'Your brother has come, and your father has killed the fattened calf, because he has received him back safe and sound.' But he was angry and refused to go in. His father came out and entreated him, but he answered his father, 'Look, these many years I have served you, and I never disobeyed your command, yet you never gave me a young goat, that I might celebrate with my friends. But when this son of yours came, who has devoured your property with prostitutes, you killed the fattened calf for him!' And he

*said to him, 'Son, you are always with me, and all that is
mine is yours. It was fitting to celebrate and be glad, for
this your brother was dead, and is alive; he was lost, and
is found.'"*

- *How do these illustrations represent a reversal of the
  world's value system?*
- *What do we learn about the lengths God would go to in
  order to save just one?*

While the world may say the 99 sheep are clearly more
valuable, Jesus was deeply concerned about the one; while
the nine coins seem to be enough, Jesus was still very much
focused on the one; while a brother still remained at home,
Jesus sought out the one who needed to be brought back.

Jesus always carried a great burden for the masses but never
neglected the importance of each individual He encountered.
He set out to change the world and in many ways did so one
person at a time.

READ:

Luke 19:1-5 —

*He entered Jericho and was passing through. And behold,
there was a man named Zacchaeus. He was a chief tax
collector and was rich. And he was seeking to see who
Jesus was, but on account of the crowd he could not,
because he was small in stature. So he ran on ahead and
climbed up into a sycamore tree to see him, for he was
about to pass that way. And when Jesus came to the place,
he looked up and said to him, "Zacchaeus, hurry and come
down, for I must stay at your house today."*

Mark 5:21-34 —

And when Jesus had crossed again in the boat to the other side, a great crowd gathered about him, and he was beside the sea. Then came one of the rulers of the synagogue, Jairus by name, and seeing him, he fell at his feet and implored him earnestly, saying, "My little daughter is at the point of death. Come and lay your hands on her, so that she may be made well and live." And he went with him.

And a great crowd followed him and thronged about him. And there was a woman who had had a discharge of blood for twelve years, and who had suffered much under many physicians, and had spent all that she had, and was no better but rather grew worse. She had heard the reports about Jesus and came up behind him in the crowd and touched his garment. For she said, "If I touch even his garments, I will be made well." And immediately the flow of blood dried up, and she felt in her body that she was healed of her disease. And Jesus, perceiving in himself that power had gone out from him, immediately turned about in the crowd and said, "Who touched my garments?" And his disciples said to him, "You see the crowd pressing around you, and yet you say, 'Who touched me?'" And he looked around to see who had done it. But the woman, knowing what had happened to her, came in fear and trembling and fell down before him and told him the whole truth. And he said to her, "Daughter, your faith has made you well; go in peace, and be healed of your disease."

◆ *How do these stories reflect Jesus' concern for the individual even when the masses are crowding around Him?*

◆ *What stands out to you most in these stories? What do you appreciate most about Jesus' response?*

Making it "Small"

While fostering, adopting and caring for vulnerable children is a big deal, we must learn to scale it down and make it "small," otherwise we might get lost in its massiveness.

"Choose to do for one what you wish you could do for everyone."

– Andy Stanley

God doesn't expect us to do everything for everyone; He does expect us to do something for someone. This means you don't have to change the world for them ALL; it does mean, however, you can change the world of at least ONE.

Start with coming alongside one, loving one, caring for one and making sure that at least one knows they are valued and treasured. Start with one. Remember, behind the numbers and the stats are real kids facing real issues in need of real help.

Understanding the Need

Here are some recent statistics1 that help us understand the current orphan care landscape worldwide and right here at home:

- *According to UNICEF estimates2, there are 17,900,000 orphans who have lost both parents and are living in orphanages or on the streets and lack the care and attention required for healthy development.*

- *In the U.S., 400,540 children are living without permanent families in the foster care system. 115,000 of these children are eligible for adoption, but nearly 40% of these children will wait over three years in foster care before being adopted.*

- *Each year, over 27,000 youth "age out" of foster care without the emotional and financial support necessary to succeed.*

- *As of 2011, nearly 60,000 children in foster care in the U.S. are placed in institutions or group homes, not in traditional foster homes.*

- *The average length of time a child waits to be adopted in foster care is over three years. Roughly 55% of these children have had three or more placements. One study found that 33% of children had changed elementary schools five or more times, losing relationships and falling behind educationally.*

---

1   Source: http://www.unicef.org/sowc2013/files/SWCR2013_ENG_Lo_res_24_Apr_2013.pdf

2   Source: http://thegospelcoalition.org/blogs/tgc/2013/11/07/9-things-you-should-know-about-orphans/

The statistics are daunting: millions of children around the world - hundreds of thousands within the United States, dozens of thousands within your state and city, hundreds and thousands within your community alone - needing a caring family, a safe place to call home, parents to love them and someone to tell them they matter and that everything is going to be okay. But with numbers like that it's hard to wrap our minds around what to do, where to go and how to even begin to be a solution to the problem. We must learn to "shrink" it into terms we can understand and respond to.

Every number represents a child – a real child with a real story in need of real help. We must always keep our perspective in this place. We may never change the whole world for every child, but we can at least change the world of one child.

There are No "Justs" or "Onlys" in Foster Care and Adoption

At the heart of the gospel is a radically pursuing God who goes to extravagant lengths for the sake of one. He's a God that scripture says will flip a house upside down in order to find one lost coin (Luke 15:8-10), would leave the 99 in order to chase down one lost sheep (Luke 15:3-7), would pause in a mob-like crowd to speak into the life of one struggling woman (Mark 5:24-29), would spend days traveling to heal one sick little girl (Matthew 9:18-26), would throw a lavish party for one lost son who has now been found (Luke 15:11-32).

This is the never-ending and always-pursuing love of God, systematically changing the entire landscape of humanity one.individual.person.at.a.time. We don't discredit His pursuit of one, but instead celebrate Him all the more because of it. How can the Creator of the entire universe be so intimately in tune to and concerned with the needs of one? Beautiful.

This is the heart of God decisively demonstrated through the gospel – He is consequentially concerned with the whole, but never to the neglect of the one.

There are no "justs" or "onlys" in foster care and adoption. You won't "just" foster a few or "only" adopt one. You won't "just" support families or "only" serve in other helpful ways. Instead, everything you do has the capacity to significantly alter the future trajectory of a child's life forever. Generations to come will never be the same. That's so much bigger than "just" or "only".

- ♦ *In what ways, if any, have you already begun to feel the temptation to compare yourself to what others are doing?*

- ♦ *Why is it important to understand that there are no "justs" or "onlys" in this? What freedom does that offer you?*

DISCUSS

As you close your time together, spend 5-10 minutes processing the things you have learned and discussed. This is an especially important opportunity to share thoughts, feelings, questions, concerns or any resolutions you have made in response to your study.

- ◆ *What truth or idea stood out to you most in this session? Why?*

- ◆ *Why is it important for us to not get so overwhelmed with the great need out there?*

- ◆ *What do the truths and ideas discussed in the session make you think about your own calling to care for the marginalized, abused and neglected?*

REFLECT

As you reflect on the truths of this session and consider the personal implications for your own life, spend some time writing and processing through the following three questions:

1. *How does "shrinking the problem" help you think through what role you can play in caring for vulnerable children and families?*

2. *What impact do you hope to make on the life of at least one child? What things do you want them to be able to say about your involvement in their life as they grow up?*

3. *Consider the legacy you can leave and the generational impact you can make on the life of one child. What thoughts, dreams, fears and joys come to mind? What excites you the most about the possibilities?*

REFLECTIVE WRITING

_____

_____

_____

_____

_____

_____

_____

_____

_____

_____

_____

_____

_____

_____

_____

_____

_____

_____

_____

_____

_____

_____

_____

_____

ADDITIONAL SCRIPTURE TO USE IN PRAYER:

John 10:4; Ephesians 4:1–16; Romans 12:4–6; 1 Peter 4:10

HEAD: *What biblical truth did you learn from this?*

_____

_____

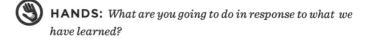

HEART: *What do the ideas we are discussing make you think and feel?*

_____

_____

HANDS: *What are you going to do in response to what we have learned?*

_____

_____

EVERYONE CAN DO SOMETHING

—

*We're not all called to do the same thing,
but we are all capable of doing something.*

PRAY

—

As you gather the group together, begin with prayer. Each group member should have the opportunity to share any particular requests they would like the group to pray for. Use this time as an opportunity to encourage one another and focus your hearts and minds on what God may have in store during your time together.

CONNECT

—

Spend the next 5-10 minutes connecting as a group. Catch up on what's going on in each other's lives.

- *How has your week been?*
- *Did anything out of the ordinary or particularly interesting happen?*
- *Is anything coming up for you between now and the next group meeting that you want group members to know?*

In Session 5, we talked about "shrinking" the problem doing for at least one what you wish you could do for all. During this session, we will take a biblical look at how the Body of Christ is called to operate together – with unique diversity but all for the common good. Specifically, we will look at how the Body of Christ can serve vulnerable children and families in different but equally important ways.

The Bible says every believer has been given a unique set of spiritual gifts. Have you ever identified yours?

Spiritual Gifts Survey

Before you begin this study, spend the next 10-15 minutes silently and quickly answering the questions in the Spiritual Gifts Survey at the back of the book, determining your "scores" and sharing your top 3 results with the group.

GROW

—

One Body, Many Parts

The imagery of a human body is consistently used throughout Scripture to illustrate the identity and activity of the Church – how the people of God relate with each other and work together. Ultimately, unique gifts are given to unique individuals, not for their own good but for the good of the whole body. Within the Body of Christ roles are established not on the basis of rank, as if one person's position was more important than another, but on the premise that when each member fulfills their responsibility the whole body will function better for it.

READ:

1 Corinthians 12:4-7 —

Now there are varieties of gifts, but the same Spirit; and there are varieties of service, but the same Lord; and there are varieties of activities, but it is the same God who empowers them all in everyone. To each is given the manifestation of the Spirit for the common good.

- *What stands out to you most in this passage?*
- *What do we learn about uniqueness, diversity and unity in the Body of Christ? Based on these verses, how would you define "unity"?*

READ:

1 Corinthians 12:18-19, 27 —

> *But as it is, God arranged the members in the body, each one of them, as he chose. If all were a single member, where would the body be?...Now you are the body of Christ and individually members of it.*

- *How are we to understand the role we have been given in the Body? Has God made any mistakes in giving some people certain gifts and callings and other people different ones?*
- *What does this passage communicate about the essential nature of our diverse roles?*
- *Discuss the tone of this passage. Does it seem to suggest your role in the Body is optional?*

The proper functioning of the people of God to fulfill the purposes of God are always portrayed in communal terms, not individualistic ones. Everyone has a role to play, but not everyone is called to play the same role. The call to care for the vulnerable is for all – we all have a role to play, there are no exceptions. The question is not "Am I supposed to get involved?" but rather, "HOW am I supposed to get involved?"

"Each of us has a role to play, and every role is important. There is no small service to God; it all matters."

– Rick Warren

Opportunities to Get Involved

While the call is to all, the opportunities to respond are limitless and full of possibilities. No one can do everything, but everyone can do something. You may not be called to bring a child into your home, but you can certainly play a role in serving and supporting those who do. Or perhaps you will bring children into your home on short-term arrangements while others will foster and/or adopt more long-term. Again, no one can do everything, but everyone can do something.

Here are some common, practical ways to care for vulnerable children and their families or to simply provide care and support for those who are.

Foster Care

Foster care is a temporary living arrangement for abused, neglected, and dependent children who need a safe place (homes or treatment centers) to live when their parents or another relative cannot take care of them. Foster families are recruited, trained, and licensed to care for abused and neglected children temporarily, while their parents work with social work professionals to resolve their family issues. In cases where the child becomes free for adoption, foster parents may be considered as adoptive parents.

Adoption

Adoption is a legal process that permanently gives parental rights to adoptive parents. Adoption means taking a child into your home as a permanent family member. There are opportunities to adopt through the foster care system, private domestic agencies and international agencies. Adoption finalizes a child's permanent placement into his/her new family.

Respite Care

Respite care is basically short-term foster care. It is primarily used to provide aid to other foster families needing childcare for more than 24 hours and less than 14 days. This is extremely helpful as situations often come up in which the family must travel and can't take the child due to state rules. Respite care gives foster, adoptive, and kinship parents and children the chance to have short, regular periods of time apart in which they can rest and recharge. It also provides crisis care for the times in which the trauma of the child is seriously impacting other members of the family.

Babysitting

In the world of foster care, getting a babysitter isn't the easiest thing. In fact, it's somewhat of a process. You can support foster families by becoming a certified babysitter. This allows you to provide child care for foster families so parents can have an occasional time to "get away." This is an invaluable gift to a foster family and is always much appreciated. Generally, a background check and CPR/First Aid certification are required, although many states aren't even requiring that anymore.

CASA

Court Appointed Special Advocates (CASA) volunteers are appointed by judges to watch over and advocate for abused and neglected children, to make sure they don't get overlooked by the legal and social system. In many ways, CASA advocates help speak for the child. They are of tremendous value in seeing that the child's best interests are protected.

Safe Families

Safe Families for ChildrenTM provides a temporary safe environment for children while giving the parents a chance to get back on their feet before abuse or neglect occur. Parents experiencing a temporary crisis can arrange for their children to stay with families of faith so they can manage the issues that led to their crisis situation.

Financial Supporter

Whether you're able to write a $500 check or organize fundraisers online for cash, donating to a family who wants to adopt is a much needed and very fulfilling way to answer the call to orphan care.

General Resourcing

Many foster care and adoption placements happen with little to no advance notice. This usually means that needs can come up quickly. Donations of gift cards, diapers, and new supplies such as strollers, mattresses, car seats, and other necessities are invaluable for those who are bringing children into their homes.

The following charts help you to see it visually. Imagine a family bringing children into their home, and a community of other people wrapping around them providing tangible, relational and spiritual support. *(Note: These ideas are not exhaustive, just examples.)*

EVERYONE CAN DO SOMETHING

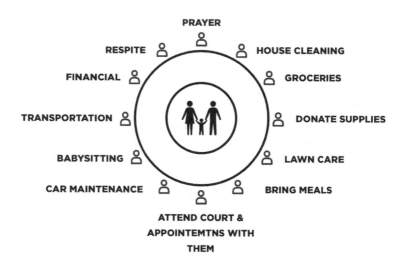

Think "Outside the Box"

Get creative! Mow foster families yards for them. Host a parents' night out for foster and adoptive couples at church. Organize back-to-school drives to collect supplies for local foster children. Throw a big Christmas party for foster families and children. Use your business or hobby as a conduit to bless children and families. The opportunities to serve, support and show appreciation are endless. Get creative!

Identifying Your "Something"

Part of discovery what God is calling you to is identifying with clarity and confidence what He's not leading you to. But how do you do that? Consider these three practical steps.

Pray. Ask God to open your heart to His, and to protect you from the tendency to rationalize and justify so that you can just obey. Be willing to say "yes" to the uncertainties and unknowns.

Share with your community. Our unique roles in the Body of Christ are given for the "common good" - the benefit of the whole body. Who better to filter our thoughts and feelings through than other members of the body? Community is a crucial filter for us in determining where and how God is leading. They can see blindspots we can't but they can also see brightspots we're unable or unwilling to see.

Research. Educate your on the various ways there are to come alongside vulnerable kids and support the families who do. Read books and blogs, attend conferences, talk to other families. You'll naturally find some opportunities are clearly not for you while others stir up a passion.

Battling the Enemies of Comparison and Guilt

Charles Swindoll once said, *"When the Lord makes it clear you're to follow Him in this new direction, focus fully on Him and refuse to be distracted by comparisons with others."* In other words, stop looking at what others are doing and just start doing what you're supposed to do.

Discuss how comparison and guilt become major distractions to our ability to find confidence in our calling?

What steps can you take to quiet the voices of comparison and guilt as you take your next best steps forward on this journey?

DISCUSS

As you close your time together, spend 5-10 minutes processing the things you have learned and discussed. This is an especially important opportunity to share thoughts, feelings, questions, concerns or any resolutions you have made in response to your study.

- *What truth or idea stood out to you most in this session? Why?*

- *Why is it important for us to not get so overwhelmed with the great need out there?*

- *What do the truths and ideas discussed in the session make you think about your own calling to care for the marginalized, abused and neglected?*

REFLECT

As you reflect on the truths of this session and consider the personal implications for your own life, spend some time writing and processing through the following three questions:

1. *How does "shrinking the problem" help you think through what role you can play in caring for vulnerable children and families?*

2. *What impact do you hope to make on the life of at least one child? What things do you want them to be able to say about your involvement in their life as they grow up?*

3. *Consider the legacy you can leave and the generational impact you can make on the life of one child. What thoughts, dreams, fears and joys come to mind? What excites you the most about the possibilities?*

REFLECTIVE WRITING

_____

_____

_____

_____

_____

_____

_____

_____

_____

_____

_____

_____

_____

_____

_____

_____

_____

_____

_____

ADDITIONAL SCRIPTURE TO USE IN PRAYER:
John 10:4; Ephesians 4:1–16; Romans 12:4–6; 1 Peter 4:10

HEAD: *What biblical truth did you learn from this?*

_____

_____

HEART: *What do the ideas we are discussing make you think and feel?*

_____

_____

HANDS: *What are you going to do in response to what we have learned?*

_____

_____

–

YOUR BEST NEXT STEP

–

Jason Johnson

We all have an "inner voice" that sometimes whispers to us and sometimes screams at us. Mine is usually preaching a message of fear and doubt when I sense God leading me in a certain direction. Maybe yours is too. It's asking, "Who are you to think you can make a difference?" or "What if you don't have what it takes?" or "What if you fail and look foolish to others?" or "Are you sure you've heard correctly from God on this?" Your voice could be asking you a million other things right now. That's the thing about these voices; they're as distinct and unique as each individual person. Like a fingerprint on your conscious – whispering, sometimes screaming.

As you wrap up this study, what's yours saying to you?

If you're like our family when we were in the very beginning stages of starting our foster care and adoption journey, you've got a mash-up of excitement and fear, eagerness and doubt, hope and worry playing in your head. Yet somehow, it's the fear and doubt and worry that often seem the loudest – and the most paralyzing. They're also incredibly sneaky – disguising themselves at times as valid, logical reasons why it might not be the right time, why we might not be cut out for this, or why we don't in fact have what it takes to do this. Fear and doubt and worry want to convince you that no matter what, you shouldn't do this.

So how do we confront this? What's our strategy? To truly quiet the voices (notice I did not say silence...I'm not sure if they ever fully go away) I am increasingly convinced that we must correctly identify the root of our concern before we can adequately address the fruit of it. Let me explain...

For example, "I'm afraid of getting too attached" is the fruit; "I fear I don't have what it takes to grieve like that" is the root. Or, "I'm afraid of the effect it might have on my bio kids" is the root; "I'm afraid I don't have what it takes to parent through that" is the root. Or, "I'm afraid of my life being controlled by a child welfare system" is the fruit; "I fear I don't have what it takes to give up control like that" is the root. Or, "I'm afraid of the financial cost we will incur if we adopt" is the root; "I'm afraid I don't have what it takes to sacrifice like that" is the root.

We could go on, but you get the point.

I've shared on the blog (www.jasonjohnsonblog.com) about my own journey, and how my wife was ready to start fostering before I was. It's not that I didn't want to - it's just that I struggled with the timing. I was overwhelmed and exhausted with leading our young and busy church plant. I used the age of our three daughters as an excuse – the youngest was barely two at the time. And I searched and searched but failed to find any magical trees in our backyard growing money. Could we even afford more kids in the house right now? My inner voice was working overtime.

Looking back, I see now these were all symptoms of a much deeper, more hidden fear – they were fruits of the fear that I didn't have what it would take…to lead our church well while doing this, to be the dad my daughters needed through this, and to trust God with the details – even the financial ones – in all of this.

My inner voice sometimes whispered but mostly shouted "NO! You don't have what it takes." Maybe yours does too.

The good news is that God doesn't invite us into this expecting that we will always have "what it takes", but He does bring us into this promising that when we don't, He still does. That's our hope and assurance - that what's completely out of our capacity and control is absolutely in His.

No matter where you are – whether just now considering getting involved with this or swimming neck deep in the trenches of it already - don't let the fear of not having "what it takes" deter you from what's next, but let the confidence of Him having what it does drive you. Be free from the burden to be something for these kids only Jesus intended Himself to be. These kids don't need you to have all it takes, they just need you to be willing to try, to fail at times and to keep moving forward with them and for them. They need you to be strong enough to be weak, and to trust that in some counterintuitive way that scripture speaks to, that's ultimately where true strength is found. (2 Corinthians 12:9) Our weakness is no longer an excuse, but is now a platform upon which the power of God can be made most visible. It's no longer a place of "no", but now, in the gospel, becomes the place we can declare with confidence, "I'm not sure how I'm going to handle all of this, but…yes."

In the end, success in foster care and adoption is not dependent upon your capacity to produce a certain set of ideal outcomes, but rather is defined by your willingness to say yes, and to trust Him with the rest. Your "yes" is your success; everything that follows is the mercy of God.

So how do you know if you're "called", "ready" or that "it's time"? When you know just enough to be afraid of it but too much to let fear have the final say about it. This means we don't wait for fear or worry to subside before we act; we simply choose to fight forward so that fear loses and kids and families win. What if we started to assume the answer was "yes" until we heard a "no", rather than "no" until we heard a "yes"? A lot would change. In the end, obedience is less about what we think we can and cannot do, and our natural inclination to avoid hard and inconvenient things, and more about what we know God wants us to do – even if it's hard and inconvenient.

We can do hard and inconvenient things. We can do scary things. We really can. But we can do those things in small, simple and strategic ways.

So now what? What's your next best simple step?

It might look like a much-needed conversation with your husband or wife that is less resistant and more receptive to the idea than you have been in the past. It could be registering for the next orientation class - no strings attached - just going to listen, learn and feel. Maybe it's grabbing coffee with another person or couple that has fostered or adopted just to hear and learn from their story. Or perhaps it's finally giving into what you've known has been true for quite some time - you just need to say yes and do it. Stop praying about it (*yep, I said that*), stop reading about it (*except at www.jasonjohnsonblog.com* ☺), stop doing studies about it (*Ha! See what I did there?*), stop talking about the "what ifs" or the "maybe one days" - and just do it.

Just take your next best steps.

Don't worry right now about the many, many other steps that will come after that. Don't be so afraid of what's to come along the journey that you never actually end up starting it. Just focus on what's next. That's the best you can do, all anyone (*especially yourself*) can really expect of you, and honestly, that's all that God is asking of you - to take the next best step...and to trust Him with the rest.

So, what's next?...

I'm excited for you,

Jason Johnson
jasonjohnsonblog.com

APPENDIX

–

SPIRITUAL GIFTS SURVEY

–

DIRECTIONS

—

This is not a test, so there are no wrong answers. The **Spiritual Gifts Survey** consists of 80 statements. Some items reflect concrete actions; other items are descriptive traits; and still others are statements of belief.

- ◆ *Select the one response you feel best characterizes yourself and place that number in the blank provided. Record your answer in the blank beside each item.*

- ◆ *Do not spend too much time on any one item. Remember, it is not a test. Usually your immediate response is best.*

- ◆ *Please give an answer for each item. Do not skip any items.*

- ◆ *Do not ask others how they are answering or how they think you should answer.*

- ◆ *Work at your own pace.*

Your response choices are:

5—Highly characteristic of me/definitely true for me

4—Most of the time this would describe me/be true for me

3—Frequently characteristic of me/true for me-about 50 percent of the time

2—Occasionally characteristic of me/true for me-about 25 percent of the time

1—Not at all characteristic of me/definitely untrue for me

_____ 1. I have the ability to organize ideas, resources, time, and people effectively.

_____ 2. I am willing to study and prepare for the task of teaching.

_____ 3. I am able to relate the truths of God to specific situations.

_____ 4. I have a God-given ability to help others grow in their faith.

_____ 5. I possess a special ability to communicate the truth of salvation.

_____ 6. I have the ability to make critical decisions when necessary.

_____ 7. I am sensitive to the hurts of people.

_____ 8. I experience joy in meeting needs through sharing possessions.

_____ 9. I enjoy studying.

_____ 10. I have delivered God's message of warning and judgment.

_____ 11. I am able to sense the true motivation of persons and movements.

_____ 12. I have a special ability to trust God in difficult situations.

_____ 13. I have a strong desire to contribute to the establishment of new churches.

_____ 14. I take action to meet physical and practical needs rather than merely talking about or planning to help.

_____ 15. I enjoy entertaining guests in my home.

_____ 16. I can adapt my guidance to fit the maturity of those working with me.

_____ 17. I can delegate and assign meaningful work.

_____ 18. I have an ability and desire to teach.

_____ 19. I am usually able to analyze a situation correctly.

_____ 20. I have a natural tendency to encourage others.

_____ 21. I am willing to take the initiative in helping other Christians grow in their faith.

_____ 22. I have an acute awareness of the emotions of other people, such as loneliness, pain, fear, and anger.

_____ 23. I am a cheerful giver.

_____ 24. I spend time digging into facts.

_____ 25. I feel that I have a message from God to deliver to others.

_____ 26. I can recognize when a person is genuine/honest.

_____ 27. I am a person of vision (a clear mental portrait of a preferable future given by God). I am able to communicate vision in such a way that others commit to making the vision a reality.

_____ 28. I am willing to yield to God's will rather than question and waver.

_____ 29. I would like to be more active in getting the gospel to people in other lands.

_____ 30. It makes me happy to do things for people in need.

_____ 31. I am successful in getting a group to do its work joyfully.

_____ 32. I am able to make strangers feel at ease.

_____ 33. I have the ability to plan learning approaches.

_____ 34. I can identify those who need encouragement.

_____ 35. I have trained Christians to be more obedient disciples of Christ.

_____ 36. I am willing to do whatever it takes to see others come to Christ.

_____ 37. I am attracted to people who are hurting.

_____ 38. I am a generous giver.

_____ 39. I am able to discover new truths.

_____ 40. I have spiritual insights from Scripture concerning issues and people that compel me to speak out.

_____ 41. I can sense when a person is acting in accord with God's will.

_____ 42. I can trust in God even when things look dark.

_____ 43. I can determine where God wants a group to go and help it get there.

_____ 44. I have a strong desire to take the gospel to places where it has never been heard.

_____ 45. I enjoy reaching out to new people in my church and community.

_____ 46. I am sensitive to the needs of people.

_____ 47. I have been able to make effective and efficient plans for accomplishing the goals of a group.

_____ 48. I often am consulted when fellow Christians are struggling to make difficult decisions.

_____ 49. I think about how I can comfort and encourage others in my congregation.

_____ 50. I am able to give spiritual direction to others.

_____ 51. I am able to present the gospel to lost persons in such a way that they accept the Lord and His salvation.

_____ 52. I possess an unusual capacity to understand the feelings of those in distress.

_____ 53. I have a strong sense of stewardship based on the recognition that God owns all things.

_____ 54. I have delivered to other persons messages that have come directly from God.

_____ 55. I can sense when a person is acting under God's leadership.

_____ 56. I try to be in God's will continually and be available for His use.

_____ 57. I feel that I should take the gospel to people who have different beliefs from me.

_____ 58. I have an acute awareness of the physical needs of others.

_____ 59. I am skilled in setting forth positive and precise steps of action.

_____ 60. I like to meet visitors at church and make them feel welcome.

_____ 61. I explain Scripture in such a way that others understand it.

_____ 62. I can usually see spiritual solutions to problems.

_____ 63. I welcome opportunities to help people who need comfort, consolation, encouragement, and counseling.

_____ 64. I feel at ease in sharing Christ with nonbelievers.

_____ 65. I can influence others to perform to their highest God-given potential.

_____ 66. I recognize the signs of stress and distress in others.

_____ 67. I desire to give generously and unpretentiously to worthwhile projects and ministries.

_____ 68. I can organize facts into meaningful relationships.

_____ 69. God gives me messages to deliver to His people.

_____ 70. I am able to sense whether people are being honest when they tell of their religious experiences.

_____ 71. I enjoy presenting the gospel to persons of other cultures and backgrounds.

_____ 72. I enjoy doing little things that help people.

_____ 73. I can give a clear, uncomplicated presentation.

_____ 74. I have been able to apply biblical truth to the specific needs of my church.

_____ 75. God has used me to encourage others to live Christlike lives.

_____ 76. I have sensed the need to help other people become more effective in their ministries.

_____ 77. I like to talk about Jesus to those who do not know Him.

_____ 78. I have the ability to make strangers feel comfortable in my home.

_____ 79. I have a wide range of study resources and know how to secure information.

_____ 80. I feel assured that a situation will change for the glory of God even when the situation seem impossible.

SCORING YOUR SURVEY

Follow these directions to figure your score for each spiritual gift.

- *Place in each box your numerical response (1-5) to the item number which is indicated below the box.*

- *For each gift, add the numbers in the boxes and put the total in the TOTAL box.*

LEADERSHIP						
	Item 6	Item 16	Item 27	Item 43	Item 65	TOTAL
ADMINISTRATION						
	Item 1	Item 17	Item 31	Item 47	Item 59	TOTAL
TEACHING						
	Item 2	Item 18	Item 33	Item 61	Item 73	TOTAL
KNOWLEDGE						
	Item 9	Item 24	Item 39	Item 68	Item 79	TOTAL
WISDOM						
	Item 3	Item 19	Item 48	Item 62	Item 74	TOTAL
PROPHECY						
	Item 10	Item 25	Item 40	Item 54	Item 69	TOTAL
DISCERNMENT						
	Item 11	Item 26	Item 41	Item 55	Item 70	TOTAL
EXHORTATION						
	Item 20	Item 34	Item 49	Item 63	Item 75	TOTAL
SHEPHERDING						
	Item 4	Item 21	Item 35	Item 50	Item 76	TOTAL
FAITH						
	Item 12	Item 28	Item 42	Item 56	Item 80	TOTAL
EVANGELISM						
	Item 5	Item 36	Item 51	Item 64	Item 77	TOTAL

APOSTLESHIP						
	Item 13	Item 29	Item 44	Item 57	Item 71	TOTAL
SERVICE/HELPS						
	Item 14	Item 30	Item 46	Item 58	Item 72	TOTAL
MERCY						
	Item 7	Item 22	Item 37	Item 52	Item 66	TOTAL
GIVING						
	Item 8	Item 23	Item 38	Item 53	Item 67	TOTAL
HOSPITALITY						
	Item 15	Item 32	Item 45	Item 60	Item 78	TOTAL

Now that you have completed the survey, thoughtfully answer the following questions.

The gifts I have begun to discover in my life are:

1. _____

2. _____

3. _____

___ Leadership   ___ Shepherding

___ Administration   ___ Faith

___ Teaching   ___ Evangelism

___ Knowledge   ___ Apostleship

___ Wisdom   ___ Service/Helps

___ Prophecy   ___ Mercy

___ Discernment   ___ Giving

___ Exhortation   ___ Hospitality

JASON JOHNSON

—

Jason and his wife, Emily, became foster parents in 2012. They live in Texas with their four daughters and enjoy whatever it is they are doing, as long as it's together.

Jason is a writer and speaker who encourages families and equips churches in their foster care and adoption journeys. He also provides consulting for church and organizational leadership teams on strategic planning and effective engagement practices in the foster care, adoption, orphan care, and justice spheres.

After growing up in a ministry home in Dallas, Texas, Jason attended Texas A&M University, where he and Emily met (Whoop!). During college Jason began working at a church, and after graduating in 2002 he began his pastoral ministries studies at Dallas Theological Seminary, while engaged in full-time ministry. In 2008, alongside a core team of people in the North Houston area, Jason had the privilege of planting and leading a church within the Acts29 Network, through which he cofounded a nonprofit organization committed to serving, supporting, and equipping foster and adoptive families in the city of Houston.

In 2013, equipped with fourteen years of church-based ministry and nonprofit leadership experience, as well as his insights from his own family's foster and adoptive journey, Jason began working for an organization helping church leaders implement structures and strategies related to foster care and adoption ministry within their churches and developing resources to encourage and support families along their journeys.

Jason speaks and teaches at churches, conferences, forums, and workshops around the country on church- based ministry strategies and best practices, and encourages families that are in the trenches and those that are considering getting involved. Much of his time is spent coaching and consulting with church leadership teams on how to implement, lead, and develop strategic and sustainable ministries within their church.

Jason is the author of *ReFraming Foster Care* and *Everyone Can Do Something* and blogs regularly at *jasonjohnsonblog.com.*

CONNECT WITH JASON HERE:

WEBSITE: *jasonjohnsonblog.com*
CONTACT: *info@jasonjohnsonblog.com*
SPEAKING REQUEST: *jasonjohnsonblog.com/speakrequest*
FACEBOOK: *facebook.com/jasonjohnsonblog*
TWITTER: *twitter.com/_jasonjohnson*
INSTAGRAM: *instagram.com/jasmjohnson*

–

ADDITIONAL RESOURCES

–

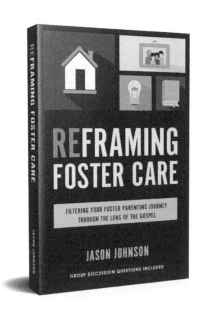

REFRAMING FOSTER CARE

Filtering Your Foster Parenting Journey
Through the Lens of the Gospel

ReFraming Foster Care is a collection of reflections on the
foster parenting journey designed to help you find hope and
remind you that your work is worth it...
and that you are not alone.

[Includes group discussion questions.]

reframingfostercare.com

EVERYONE CAN DO SOMETHING

*A Field-Guide for Strategically Rallying Your Church
Around the Orphaned and Vulnerable*

Whether you are launching a new foster care, adoption
or orphan care ministry or leading an existing one, you'll
discover the principles you need to take the next best steps
for your church, your ministry and the families and children
you are serving.

everyonecandosomethingbook.com

Made in the USA
Middletown, DE
15 January 2020